A PHILOSOPHER LOOKS AT FRIENDSHIP

What is it to be a friend? What does the role of friend involve, and why? How do the obligations and prerogatives associated with that role follow on from it, and how might they mesh, or clash, with our other duties and privileges? Philosophy often treats friendship as something systematic, serious, and earnest, and much philosophical thought has gone into how 'friendship' can formally be defined. How indeed can friendship be good for us if it doesn't fit into a philosopher's neat, systematising theory of the good? For Sophie Grace Chappell, friendship is neither systematic nor earnest, yet is certainly one of the greatest goods of life. Drawing on well-known examples from popular culture and examining these alongside recent philosophical, political, social, and theological debates, Chappell demystifies and redefines friendship as a highly untidy and many-sided good, and certainly also one of the most central goods of human experience.

SOPHIE GRACE CHAPPELL is Professor of Philosophy at The Open University. Her philosophy books include *Ethics and Experience* (2009), *Knowing What to Do* (2014), *Epiphanies* (2022), and *Trans Figured* (2024). She is also a published poet (*Songs For Winter Rain*, 2021).

T0204144

A Philosopher Looks at

In this series, philosophers offer a personal and philosophical exploration of a topic of general interest.

Books in the series

A PHILOSOPHER LOOKS AT

FRIENDSHIP

SOPHIE GRACE CHAPPELL

CAMBRIDGE
UNIVERSITY PRESS

CAMBRIDGE
UNIVERSITY PRESS

Shaftesbury Road, Cambridge CB2 8EA, United Kingdom

One Liberty Plaza, 20th Floor, New York, NY 10006, USA

477 Williamstown Road, Port Melbourne, VIC 3207, Australia

314–321, 3rd Floor, Plot 3, Splendor Forum, Jasola District Centre,
New Delhi – 110025, India

103 Penang Road, #05–06/07, Visioncrest Commercial, Singapore 238467

Cambridge University Press is part of Cambridge University Press & Assessment,
a department of the University of Cambridge.

We share the University's mission to contribute to society through the pursuit of
education, learning and research at the highest international levels of excellence.

www.cambridge.org
Information on this title: www.cambridge.org/9781009255547

DOI: 10.1017/9781009255585

First published 2024 (version 2, October 2024)

Printed in Mexico by Litográfica Ingramex, S.A. de C.V., October 2024

A catalogue record for this publication is available from the British Library

Library of Congress Cataloging-in-Publication data
Names: Chappell, Sophie Grace, 1964- author.
Title: A philosopher looks at friendship / Sophie Grace Chappell.
Description: 1. | Cambridge, United Kingdom : Cambridge University Press, 2024. |
Series: A philosopher looks at | Includes bibliographical references and index.
Identifiers: LCCN 2023053448 (print) | LCCN 2023053449 (ebook) |
ISBN 9781009255547 (paperback) | ISBN 9781009255585 (ebook)
Subjects: LCSH: Friendship.
Classification: LCC BJ1533.F8 C4342 2024 (print) | LCC BJ1533.F8 (ebook) |
DDC 155.9/25–dc23/eng/20240304
LC record available at https://lccn.loc.gov/2023053448
LC ebook record available at https://lccn.loc.gov/2023053449

ISBN 978-1-009-25554-7 Paperback

Cambridge University Press & Assessment has no responsibility for the persistence
or accuracy of URLs for external or third-party internet websites referred to in this
publication and does not guarantee that any content on such websites is, or will
remain, accurate or appropriate.

*For my friends
past, present, and future*

CONTENTS

CONTENTS

ACKNOWLEDGEMENTS

Thanks to Hilary Gaskin for suggesting I write *A Philosopher Looks at Friendship* in the first place, and for her patience and long-suffering ever since she asked. For advice and comments, thanks to Hilary and also to Sean Cordell, Helen de Cruz, and James Holden. Thanks also to Matthew Shelton for tracking down the John Sparrow poem in Chapter 5, and to Thomas Haynes and Marijasintha Jacob Srinivasan for their painstaking editorial work.

And for being my friends, thanks to – all of my friends, past, present, and yet to come.

Prelude: Eighteen Aphorisms

1

You could go up into the heavens, you could contemplate the whole nature of the world and the beauty of the stars from up there – but if you had no one to tell about it, your revelation would bring you no pleasure. Whereas if you did have someone, it would be the most wonderful thing ever.

> Archytas of Tarentum (430–355 BC), in Cicero, *de Amicitia* section 88

2

It is not good for man to be alone.
> Genesis 2.18

3

Any human being is like a blob of sealing-wax that has been broken into two halves: each of us is just one half of an original whole, and there is only one other half out there that he will fit with. And he spends his whole life looking for that other half.

> Aristophanes' speech in Plato, *Symposium* 191d, 192e (paraphrased)

4

A friend is another self.
Aristotle, *Nicomachean Ethics* 1166a31–32

5

Friendship can exist only between good men.

Cicero, *de Amicitia* 18

6

Only make friends with those who are better persons than you are.
Confucius, *Analects* 19.3

7

Someone with too many friends must be friendly to all of them; but there is a friend who sticks closer than a brother.
Proverbs 18.24

8

How good it is for brothers and sisters to live together in unity!
Psalm 133.1

9

To talk together, to laugh together, to do each other kind services in turn, to read sweet-written books together, to joke together and to be serious together ... this is what we love in our friends.

Augustine, *Confessions* 4.8–9

10

If someone pressed me to explain why I loved my friend, I could not express it any other way than by saying: 'Because he is himself, because I am myself.'

Michel de Montaigne, 'Of Friendship' (paraphrased)

11

A crowd is not company; and faces are but a gallery of pictures; and talk but a tinkling cymbal, where there is no love. The Latin adage meeteth with it a little: *Magna civitas, magna solitudo* [great city, great aloneness]; because in a great town friends are scattered; so that there is not that fellowship, for the most part, which is in less neighbourhoods. But we may go further, and affirm most truly, that it is a mere and miserable solitude to want true friends; without which the world is but a wilderness; and even in this sense also of solitude, whosoever in the frame of his nature and affections, is unfit for friendship, he taketh it of the beast, and not from humanity.

Sir Francis Bacon, 'Of Friendship'

12

Friend, n. One joined to another in mutual benevolence and intimacy.

Dr Samuel Johnson, *Johnson's Dictionary Online*

13

True love's the gift which God has given
To man alone beneath the heaven:
It is not fantasy's hot fire,
Whose wishes, soon as granted, fly;
It liveth not in fierce desire,
With dead desire it doth not die;
It is the secret sympathy,
The silver link, the silken tie,
Which heart to heart, and mind to mind,
In body and in soul can bind.
Walter Scott, 'The Lay of the Last Minstrel'

14

Friendship is far more tragic than love. It lasts longer.

Oscar Wilde (1894)

15

That outlook which values the collective above the individual necessarily disparages friendship; it is a relation between [people] at their highest degree of individuality.

C. S. Lewis (1960, 57)

16

If I had to choose between betraying my country and betraying my friend, I hope I should have the guts to betray my country.

E. M. Forster (1939, 8)

17

Can you imagine us years from today
Sharing a park bench quietly?
How terribly strange to be seventy

Simon and Garfunkel, 'Old Friends'

18

Greater love has no man than this, that he lay down his life for his friends.

John 15.13

1 Three Friendships – and Lots of Questions

Shrek

DONKEY: Hey hey hey. Come back here. I'm not through with you yet.

SHREK: Well, I'm through with you.

DONKEY: Uh uh! You know, with you it's always *me me me*. Well guess what – now it's my turn. So you just shut up and pay attention. You are mean to me. You insult me. You don't appreciate anything I do. You're always pushing me around, or pushing me away.

SHREK: Oh yeah? Well, if I treated you so bad, how come you came back?

DONKEY: Because that's what friends do. *They forgive each other.*

(*Shrek*, Dreamworks 2001)

The award-winning children's film *Shrek* came out at just the right time (in 2001) to be a favourite with our children when they were small, for family viewing (in fact, for multi-repeat family viewing). *Shrek* is a fairy-tale animation about a sad, lonely, angry, alienated ogre in a world that rejects him for being scary, ugly, and different. With Donkey's help, Shrek has just rescued the beautiful Princess Fiona from a dragon. Since this is a fairy-tale, Shrek has of course fallen in love with Fiona, but since he is an ogre and she is (apparently) a princess, he is sure his love is in vain. He has always kept up a tough and cynical exterior, but now he has stormed off from

Princess Fiona because he has overheard her saying 'Who could love a hideous, ugly beast?' – and mistakenly assumed that she meant him.

Fiona said those painful words to Donkey. Like Shrek, Donkey is a misfit in the world of the film; their shared exclusion is the starting point of Shrek and Donkey's friendship. Now Shrek thinks that even Donkey has betrayed him – that even Donkey and Fiona are laughing at him behind his back. But Donkey goes after Shrek and confronts him to ask Shrek why he has stormed off. As the saying is, every good story has a beginning, a muddle, and an end. The dialogue that I quote comes from the turning-point in the film where the muddle is about to be resolved.

Outside fairy-tales, in the real world, it is easy to allow our society's snobbery about 'popular culture', and its weird combination of mawkish sentimentality and condescending dismissiveness about children (who after all deserve neither, given that they are simply young human beings), to blind us to the fact that many children's films provide excellent resources for thinking about big ethical questions. And that includes big ethical questions about friendship. (*Methodological note #1*: So don't ignore children's films and literature. Also, *methodological note #2*: Don't do philosophy only by referencing other philosophers. Throughout this book, I shall be careful to observe both.)

So with *Shrek*. 'That's what friends do,' says Donkey, and his words land a blow even on the harshly unidealistic Shrek. But aside from what Donkey mentions, forgiving each other, what *is* it that friends do? What is it to be a friend? Is there even one thing, actually, that it is to be a friend?

7

Some philosophers, including me, are interested in what we call *role ethics*, the study of the duties, rights, obligations, and so on that arise from occupying a role. A role here means something like *colleague* or *parent* or *lifeguard* or *firefighter* or *philosophy professor*. Friendship too seems pretty clearly to be some kind of role, with particular obligations and prerogatives and emphases and specialisations that flow from occupying the role. But if friendship *is* a role, what obligations and prerogatives does the role of friend involve, and why? How might the obligations, prerogatives, and so forth that come from one role mesh, or clash, with those that come our other roles?

Alongside the question whether friendship is a role, and if so what kind of role, there is the connected question whether FRIENDSHIP is what philosophers call a thick ethical concept. (Note: I follow a common convention among philosophers of writing the names of concepts in capitals when those concepts are particularly under scrutiny.) Thick ethical concepts are concepts like PROMISING, GENEROSITY, HONOUR, TRUST. They are, as we could call them, *bridging* concepts: that is, they are concepts that link possible courses of action in the world, via particular institutions or traditions or practices or dispositions in the world, to moral verdicts like RIGHT, WRONG, GOOD, BAD, OBLIGATORY. (The concepts named by these morally verdictive words are often called the 'thin ethical concepts'. It is a further question whether any ethical concept is entirely 'thin', entirely lacking in social and historical situatedness. Indeed it is a further question whether any naturally occurring concept at all is thin in that sense – one that I have answered 'No', in an essay called 'There Are No Thin Concepts' (Chappell 2013). But certainly only some concepts play the bridging role just outlined between descriptions of the world and practical deliberations.)

So thick ethical concepts can be a key connecting factor in moral explanations and moral justifications. For instance, my practical reasoning (explicit or inexplicit) might say: 'I must give these books back before Christmas, because I PROMISED' (using capitals as noted above). Or: 'That was a good thing to do because it was GENEROUS.' Or: 'She felt obliged to resign as a matter of HONOUR.' Or: 'It was particularly bad to leave the dog in kennels so long when she was just beginning to TRUST you.'

Now it seems clear that we can use role-descriptions in something like the same way. For example: 'I am a lifeguard, so I must dive in the water right now.' To dive in the water is my duty, my obligation, something it would be wrong for me not to do. How so? Because there are people out there in the water right now who, as the newspapers say, have got into difficulty, and because I am a lifeguard. So here the role of LIFEGUARD is the key link between a situation-description and an action-prescription for me.

It also seems clear that we can use FRIENDSHIP in this sort of explanatory way. Consider again Donkey's ringing affirmation, 'That's what friends do', in the quotation above. Given the capitalising convention that I have mentioned, it looks like we should rewrite this as 'That's what FRIENDS do.' Apparently friendship too is both a role *and* a thick ethical concept. And more generally, it seems that the names of most roles are typically thick concepts. PARENT certainly behaves like a thick concept, as when people say things like 'I care because I'm your mother' or 'You're my father, you're supposed to be there for me.'

Come to that, it has often been argued that MAN and WOMAN are thick ethical concepts too, and roles as well. A whole host of song lyrics suggest exactly this: just to give two of the most famous examples, Bob Dylan's 'Just Like a Woman' and James Brown's 'It's a Man's World'. At a rather more cerebral level there is Simone de Beauvoir's ([1949] 1972, 1) famous aphorism, at the beginning of *The Second Sex*, that *On ne naît pas femme: on le devient* ('One is not born woman: one becomes it').

Some people read de Beauvoir's aphorism as designed to echo Jean-Jacques Rousseau's equally well-known slogan, 'Man is born free and everywhere he is in chains', *L' homme est né libre et partout il est dans les fers* (Rousseau [1762] 1913, xvi) – so that de Beauvoir's point is that the role and the concept of WOMAN, at least as we have it, is a kind of prison from which people (mainly but not exclusively the female ones) need to be liberated. They take her slogan as a call for the *abolition* of the roles of gender, just as we might take slogans like Rousseau's as a call for the abolition of roles like SLAVE. However, de Beauvoir's aphorism is also often quoted as an *approval* of the role of WOMAN, at least in some form or other: for example by those who think that 'gender is performative', and who don't think that all such performances are so pernicious that the gender roles MAN and WOMAN should be abolished altogether.

Whether or not we should be abolitionists about the role of WOMAN is not something that I will talk about here. (I talk about it a bit in another book of mine, *Trans Figured*; see Chappell 2024.) But it is worth noting something that the example vividly teaches us. This is that, for any role, there is not only the question of what that role involves, but also the more fundamental question of whether we should allow the role to exist in our society at all. (Consider SLAVE again. Or MAFIOSO. Or CONCENTRATION CAMP GUARD. Or, I am tempted to say with an eye on the UK specifically, PEER.)

Has anyone ever been an abolitionist about FRIENDSHIP? Yes: some people have thought that we are obliged to care equally for everyone. Friendship, they think, undermines this obligation by pointing us towards some people in particular, at the expense of others in particular. This is something that utilitarians might conceivably think, and sometimes have (more about them later). It is also something that revolutionary socialists have sometimes thought: part of the point of calling everyone 'comrade' is that under communism *everyone* is my comrade. We all hold all property in common, and all means of production, and all political power. In exactly the same way – the idea is – we all have our affections in common.

Some religious movements too have sometimes tried to abolish 'particular friendships'. Here is the American Jesuit Charles Shelton SJ:

> ... Until the post-Vatican II era, caution against
> 'particular friendship' was a common feature of Jesuit
> training. I have heard older Jesuits describe their training:

> during recreation periods, they had to walk in threes
> rather than twos, and they were expected not to spend
> too much time alone with the same companion.
> Homophobic fears and the cultural ethos of the time no
> doubt fuelled such policies, [and] because we are
> members of a religious community, a myopically held
> assumption of 'affection in common' prevailed – a sort of
> levelling of the emotional field . . . the assumption was
> that we somehow violated our common way of living if
> we wrote about or focused on specific relationships to the
> exclusion of the wider brotherhood. (1975, 4)

As Shelton adds at once, he sees a very simple problem with
any such attempt to exclude partiality:

> The problem with such a premise is, simply, that it
> doesn't work! Humans naturally desire bonded
> attachment and, depending upon the relationship, such
> attachment varies in its quality and intensity. Even in the
> 1940s and 50s, when the training was more restrictive,
> some Jesuits naturally gravitated toward certain men who
> later came to be considered close friends . . . (1975, 4)

We will come back to the ideas of partiality and universal
benevolence in Chapter 2, when we look at utilitarianism.

For now, let's proceed on the working assumption
that friendship is a thick ethical concept, and not one (like
SLAVE or MAFIOSO or perhaps WOMAN) that we simply
want to abolish. If so, then it must be worthwhile to ask
exactly how the thick concept FRIENDSHIP works, and
what exactly it implies for our actions and decisions.
It must be a good idea to look around and think when and
where we can appeal to friendship in explanations of good

and bad, right and wrong. When is it on-target to say 'I should do this for you *because you are my friend*'? And when isn't it on-target? Why is it correct to make that appeal sometimes, and in other places either irrelevant, or positively inappropriate? We all have (or most of us have) an instinctive *feel* for right and wrong uses of such an appeal. It would be interesting to understand better what justifies that feel, or proves it to be unjustified after all.

Here many philosophers will hope for something *simple and unifying* that justifies the feeling that we are right (or wrong) to appeal to friendship in any given case. Philosophers who hope for this are buying into the ambition of the systematising theorist, who hopes to find a straightforward pattern of explanation that works all over the place. Myself I am, as we shall see, pretty sceptical about the systematising ambition. Of course it is nice if things that look complicated turn out to be simple. But I see no special reason to think that they will always or even often do so, in ethics any more than in, say, physics. Given the immense complexity of human life, there is every reason to expect the ethics of human life to be complex too. But if it is one kind of progress to come to see a simple justification for complicated phenomena, it is also progress, of a different kind, to come to see why no such simple justification is available. Maybe, by the end of this book, we will have made a little progress of both kinds.

When Harry Met Sally

A second American comedy film that also raises big philosophical questions about friendship is *When Harry Met*

Sally. Here the questions are about friendship and romance. Or perhaps I mean friendship *versus* romance:

HARRY: You realise, of course, that we can never be friends.

SALLY: Why not?

HARRY: What I'm saying is – and this is not a come-on in any way, shape, or form – is that men and women can't be friends because the sex part always gets in the way.

SALLY: That's not true. I have a number of men friends and there is no sex involved.

HARRY: No you don't. You only think you do.

SALLY: You're saying I'm having sex with these men without my knowledge?

HARRY: No, what I'm saying is they all *want* to have sex with you.

SALLY: How do you know?

HARRY: Because no man can be friends with a woman that he finds attractive. He always wants to have sex with her.

SALLY: Well, I guess we're not going to be friends then.

HARRY: Guess not.

> (*When Harry Met Sally*, Columbia 1989, screenplay by Nora Ephron; my quotation is slightly edited)

The brash young Harry's crude and dogmatic assertions are offensive in more than one way. For one thing, they are intrusively personal about Sally's private life, and involve him in an unamiable amount of 'mansplaining' her own relationships to her. For another, it is hard to warm to Harry's airy assumption that all people are either heterosexual men or heterosexual women (and indeed that all people are either men or women). But looking beyond these objections, Harry is raising a batch of really interesting questions.

Not all societies have thought that friendship does conflict with sexual/romantic involvement (whether gay or straight or something else). There have been plenty of societies where friendship quite often meant a relationship between an older man and a younger man that normally did involve homosexual flirtation at the very least, and quite often physical sex acts as well: the Azande of central Africa, traditional Japan, and Plato's Athens are all examples. (Under what circumstances a younger Athenian man should let an older man have his wicked way with him, and what exactly 'having his way with him' might involve, was in Plato's time a question for endless and no doubt enjoyably titillating debate. These debates are sometimes reflected in Plato's dialogues, for example in the *Phaedrus*, *Charmides*, and *Symposium*.)

So exactly why do so many people say today what Harry says to Sally: that friendship and romance inevitably conflict? Is the idea that romance *destroys* friendship, or just that romance *replaces* friendship? Or is it, as C. S. Lewis once suggested (more about him in Chapter 8), because our society is so segregated by sex that men and women in our society mostly don't have enough in common for friendships between them even to be possible?

Given the high prestige and value that our society accords to romance and sex, we might think that if a friendship transmutes into a romance, no serious loss is involved anyway – maybe, in fact, something more like a gain. Certainly, when a friendship *doesn't* turn into a romance, we often see that as a failure – at least if it is a man/woman friendship. We more or less expect a film that involves a man–woman partnership of some kind – such as *When Harry Met Sally*, and indeed *Shrek* – to end in a romance, and we tend to feel a bit cheated if it doesn't. Similarly, both in films and in real life, when a woman (as it usually is) tells a man (as it usually is) 'Let's just be friends', she is usually not giving him a boost, but deflating him.

(*Heteronormativity sidebar*: As a rule we have no such expectation about fictional same-sex partnerships, especially not if (as is usual) they are male. No one feels *cheated* that Holmes and Watson, or Starsky and Hutch, or Morse and Lewis, never end up as lovers. Indeed many people will find the very idea of these pairs as lovers as bizarre and comical as the idea of Morecambe and Wise in bed together. They may also, interestingly enough, find that suggestion threatening. Perhaps this fact about common attitudes in our society gives us a clue that heteronormativity is much more pervasive than it might look to be.)

Maybe it is possible to do what people often advise us to do, and 'marry your best friend'. Some of us think we have done exactly that. But if you do marry your best friend, do you thereby extinguish your friendship with them? Or your romance? Or both? It might be correct to think of friend and boyfriend/girlfriend as different roles – and husband/wife as different roles again. It doesn't seem so clear that these roles, if that is what they are, must always exclude each other. Or if they do, some people have sometimes thought that the role of the friend is more important than that of the lover:

> Marriage with anyone who I don't think the most
> splendid friend I've ever had doesn't interest me. Love
> and sex are very fine, but they won't last. Friendship – the
> kind of friendship I am talking about – is charity and

loving-kindness more than it's sex and it lasts as long as life. What's more, it grows, and sex dwindles: has to. So – will you marry me and be friends? We'll have love and we'll have sex, but we won't build on those alone. You don't have to answer now. But I wish you'd think very seriously about it, because if you say no ... I don't have to crawl and whine and pretend I can't live without you. I can, and if I must, I'll do it. But I can live so much better with you, and you can live so much better with me ...
(Davies 1981, 311)

By the end of *When Harry Met Sally*, it does look (if you'll forgive the plot-spoiler) like Harry and Sally have both been proved right, in a way. Sally is proved right that a man and a woman can be friends for decades without also being romantically involved, because she and Harry are. But Harry is proved right that friends like them are almost bound to get romantically involved in the end – because he and Sally do. And apparently, they do both end up married to their best friend.

High Fidelity

A third piece of popular culture that we might use for thinking about friendship – and sex and romance too – is Nick Hornby's grimly funny north-London novel *High Fidelity* (1995). A good way to get across what is going on in *High Fidelity* is to use two brief quotations from reviews of the book:

A very funny and concise explanation of why we men are as we are. If you are male, you should read it and then make your partner read it, so that they will no longer hate you but pity you instead. (Harry Enfield, in *The Independent on Sunday*, quoted as a blurb on the back of the paperback)

I have known quite a few men like Rob Fleming, the central character of Nick Hornby's first novel. Men who not only look for but find the meaning of life in a sleeve note or a chord change in a Pretenders song. Men who believe that the only reliable way to glimpse the soul of another is via their record collection.

I have spent nights celebrating such men's 33 1/3rd birthdays – 33 1/3, because when all is said and done such men would really rather be a piece of vinyl than a human being. In Vinyl-land, you get to rub shoulders with the other great pieces of vinyl. You don't have to relate to those other kind of people, the ones who for some reason don't choose to define themselves in this way – women.

You see, Rob and his friends, Barry and Dick, who work in Rob's second-hand record shop, know that what really matters is what you like, not what you are like. They make endless lists of records, films, episodes of *Cheers*, in order to prove themselves to each other. In *Fever Pitch* (1992), Hornby brilliantly charted the intimate dynamics of fandom long before the vogue for Fantasy Football. In *High Fidelity*, Rob and his mates are experts at Fantasy Compilation Albums, Fantasy Soundtracks for Fantasy Lives.

In real life, Rob is 36. His girlfriend, Laura, has left him, prompting some sort of mid-life crisis ... So Rob does what a man's gotta do and rearranges his record collection ... (Suzanne Moore, *The Guardian*, 28 March 1995)

If you read *High Fidelity*, one of the things that grabs you straight away about Rob, Barry, and Dick is how rubbish all three of them are at both romance and friendship. Not only are these three men (all default cis-heterosexuals) ham-fisted, inarticulate, and basically lost with women; they're no better with each other. If anything they're worse, because one thing Hornby's novel makes very clear is that while they have a minimal idea of what the role of boyfriend/lover/partner involves, they have no clue at all about what is involved in friendship with other men. As we might also put it: they don't understand the role of being friends with each other.

This is, if you like, another angle on a problem about role ethics that we have already touched on: the problem of the *indeterminacy* of at least some roles, including friendship. In our society today in the liberal West, we don't quite seem to know what the role of friendship is; we don't even seem entirely sure that friendship is a role at all, at least in the way that *colleague* or *parent* or *philosophy professor* is a role. Here Nick Hornby has put his finger on a genuine problem in our society. The nature of friendship, what being a friend commits us to and why, is something that is extremely unclear to most of us today. (And was there any rose-tinted Yesterday when it was *clearer*? Not necessarily.)

Hornby seems right, too, that this is a gendered problem: that it is a particular problem with friendships between men. It's simply obscure to us all, but especially to men, what they can reasonably expect or demand from their friends, and what they can reasonably expect or demand from each other. And that can make our (and especially men's) social world a dark and puzzling place.

Friendship today, we might say, is rather like Christmas. From a thousand and one books and films and songs (and advertisements), everyone knows what 'the ideal Christmas' is supposed to be like. But not many of us are content or comfortable just to buy into that ideal without reservation – not even those of us who are Christians. (Sometimes *especially* not those of us who are Christians.) There is a lot about the ideal Christmas that most of us find fraudulent, fake, silly, saccharine, or otherwise repellent. Similarly with friendship, it's not that we don't know what a friend is supposed to be like. It's more like we know only too well what a friend is meant to be like – and just find we can't endorse that ideal.

In our society there are some fairly specific rules about how to be a man friend to another man, or a woman friend to another woman, but so many people feel like rejecting these rules. You don't have to be gender non-conforming to be repelled and alienated by blokeyness, by the role of the Bloke as we might call it. Probably most intelligent and reflective male-born people find the social prescriptions involved in the Role of the Bloke pretty unattractive. Yet any man or boy who has been in a rugby team or a school cadets unit, or who will insist on watching *Top Gear* or hanging out with train-spotters or real-ale enthusiasts or detectorists, will have had blokeyness imposed on him. (Yes, of course there are female train-spotters or real-ale enthusiasts or detectorists ... all the same.) In these contexts at least, male friendship is a very well-defined role, involving, let us say, an inordinate interest in malt whisky, engines, muscular sports, loud music, military history, and more or less explicit photographs of very beautiful women. (Another observation from *High Fidelity*: male friendship seems to involve a lot of compiling lists, too.) But for lots of men, this set of stereotypes causes them nothing but discomfort. Understandably enough, they reject *this* version of the role of male friendship; having rejected this, and found no obvious alternative version, they end up in the same state of confusion about what friendship can be for men as Rob, Barry, and Dick are in in Hornby's novel.

It is an interesting question what corresponding rules and stereotypes our society imposes on the role of friendship for women. The pressures here seem real enough, and in some ways worse. Of course some almost parodic versions of what it is for women to be friends with each other have had plenty of publicity – see *Mamma Mia* or *Absolutely Fabulous* or *Mean Girls* or all those women's magazines and story-books for girls. In some ways these stereotypes for women's friendships might remind us of the kinds of stereotypes for men that we were looking at before; with these stereotypes too, it is only too intelligible if individual women or girls find them stiflingly and uncomfortably alien.

But in the female case there is a further problem in a society like ours, where so many things are, ultimately, organised for and around men. This is that a lot of our society's stereotypes for women are not about how women present themselves *to each other*; they are about how women present themselves, individually or in groups, *to men*. And this of course is another reason for rebelling against the stereotypes.

Whether or not our friendships comply with male or female stereotypes, there is always a further question. And this too comes up in *High Fidelity*, and *Shrek*, and *When Harry Met Sally*. This is the question of how friendship is good for us – a question that will be in the air throughout this book, and my main focus in Chapter 17.

When, that is, friendship *is* good for us, because obviously there is such a thing as a toxic friend. It would be better for Othello, and for Cassio too, if he were never friends with Iago. And with all sorts of friendships, even ones that weren't at all toxic to start with, there can, sadly, come a point at which it is either unavoidable, or clearly the right option, simply to end them. But even when my evil friends aren't actively trying to destroy me, as Iago wants to destroy both Cassio and Othello, friendship with bad people can be very bad for me. 'Bad company corrupts good character', St Paul says in 1 Corinthians 15.33 – and he is apparently quoting a Greek proverb of his day, rather like our own 'Birds of a feather'.

Naturally it's better if my friends aren't positively evil. So does that mean that only positively good people can be friends? Well, some folk wisdom suggests that being a good friend can actually conflict with being a good person: as the saying goes, 'A friend helps you move. A true friend helps you move a body.' On the other hand, many philosophers, including Plato, Aristotle, and Cicero (in my fifth aphorism in the Prelude), bring something like moral goodness right into the centre of their account of friendship. These philosophers all think that the only true friendship is the friendship of good men, adult males who are virtuous (again, notice the gendering). If you don't quite fit that ideal, whether by not being male, or not being adult, or not being good, then you are bound, at least to some extent, to miss out on friendship – at least in its highest forms, and possibly altogether.

(Corinne Gartner has the following to say on this:

> Aristotle's account of friendship in *Nicomachean Ethics* VIII–IX [is usually understood] as the locus classicus of a highly moralizing view of the phenomenon, according to which the only genuine friendships are those between two virtuous agents who are attracted to each other on the basis of moral excellence. If this conception is right, then most of our apparent friendships fail to make the cut, and most of us are, strictly speaking, friendless. (2022, 35)

Plato seems open to Gartner's criticism too: see *Lysis* 214c ff.)

Another idea about friendship that we have all heard is the idea that friendships can have a big effect on our own moral character. It is a commonplace of journalism and gossip to say that someone 'was all right until he got in with the wrong crowd'. And it is a central idea in many novels of school life – right back to *Tom Brown's Schooldays* – that friendship is a morally risky business, because we are all so prone to accept or absorb the values of the other human beings around us in our peer group.

A more sombre example than school stories is the case of Nazi Germany. Hitler's regime, no doubt, was one of the things on E. M. Forster's mind when he wrote in 1938, in my sixteenth aphorism, that he would rather betray his country than his friends. But the Nazis understood the power of peer pressure, the social forces whereby people are made to go along with what is generally accepted by the friends around them, and used it to striking effect as a way of getting German citizens in the 1930s to sign up for far more than the minimum public expressions of commitment to that monstrous regime that they could safely get away with. (A remarkable film about this chilling phenomenon is *Good* (Goldcrest Films 2008), with Jason Isaacs as a Jewish Berliner whose non-Jewish friend (Viggo Mortensen), in the interest of fitting in and avoiding risk, slowly but surely betrays him, all the way down the line to the death-camp.) Given all these dark possibilities, we might wonder what someone would be missing if they never had *any* friends. Is it really so terrible to live the life of Johnny-no-mates, as it's called in the British Army? Why couldn't a solitary get whatever benefits friendship has in some other, perhaps less risky, way?

So for a lot of philosophers, asking 'What is the benefit of friendship?' has often morphed into an adjacent inquiry: about whether friendship (or a friend) is an end in itself, or just a means to some other end. (Perhaps to the end of realising virtue, or value, or utility; or again to realising ambitions, or pleasures, or just having a good time.) Lots of philosophers – most famously Kant – have been emphatic that we are morally required to treat other people 'never merely as a means, but always at the same time as an end in themselves' ([1797] 2017, 4: 439). It sounds like Kant is telling us that it is wrong to treat our friendships as a means to procuring the benefits of friendship: his rather stern advice is that we should treat our friends as valuable in themselves, and never mind what benefits we get from them. (For a more sympathetic view of Kant on friendship see Karen Stohr, 2022, especially Chapter 25, titled 'Friends and Frenemies'.)

However, both sides of his means/ends contrast are puzzling. What is it to treat you as a means? What is it to treat you as an end in yourself? And so, what is it to treat you as a means *but not merely* as a means – to treat you as both a means and an end *at the same time*? It is not just Kant who is puzzling on this problem – and rather strangely preoccupied by it. Philosophers in general do seem peculiarly prone to this worry whether, if friendship is a means to an end, that means that we are treating our friends merely instrumentally – 'using' them – by having friendships with them. And maybe it's not just philosophers who are puzzled about this. 'I only hang out with you because you're fun. If you *weren't* fun, or stopped being fun, I'd find someone else, and quickly': we do quite often think such things. (If we're rude enough, or provoked enough, we may actually say them too.)

Another big question that philosophers have also worried about a lot arises here, about replacement or 'trading up'. If I am friends with you purely for the sake of the fun we have, but Jones would be a more fun friend than you, then why shouldn't I just dump you and hang out with Jones instead?

Philosophers of friendship call this the trading-up problem. The obvious answer (which seems like another appeal to a thick ethical concept) is: 'Because trading up would be disloyal.' But then, what is it that makes loyalty so important in a friendship? Is loyalty always the key thing, with any friend? Does it weigh the same with every friend? (The friend I met by accident in the pub three weeks ago, versus the friend I've known since primary school?) If loyalty to friends is important, then (to come back to Forster's remark) how should we balance it against other kinds of loyalty, like patriotism? Does loyalty mean that I have a duty to cling on grimly to our relationship, even though, these days, you bore me rigid? Or to pretend that you are more fun to be with than you actually are? People say of romantic relationships that 'Love is blind', but maybe friendship is blind too sometimes – maybe friends miss each other's faults through bias and partiality.

Speaking of partiality, here is another ethical problem that arises at once when we think about friendship. When is it morally permissible to be partial or biased towards my friends, and when not? I can choose to invite you to my party, but not Jones, because you are my friend and Jones isn't. So why can't I choose to give you the job, and not Jones, because you are my friend and Jones isn't? What, in short, is the difference between friendship and cronyism, and how do we draw a line between them?

Here we can appeal again to roles. When I appoint someone to a job, I am acting in my professional role, and I should use the standards and the criteria dictated by that role. To appoint someone to a post where we are looking for *the best philosopher available* on the grounds that she is *my best friend available* is to fail to recognise this distinction between the different roles that I occupy, and to appoint by reference to an irrelevant standard.

This answer must be broadly correct, but it is not clear how it determines some of the more marginal cases. After all, the fact that I am good friends with someone isn't *entirely* irrelevant in the workplace; on the contrary, it usually makes our work go much better than it would if we thoroughly disliked each other. So if two candidates are tied for professional ability, and one is my friend and the other isn't, mightn't I use my friendship as a tie-breaker?

My own answer to that is 'No', partly because I think that there is too much scope for self-deception about which comparisons really are ties, and partly because I think that friendship should not be considered positively relevant even in *this* way. On the other hand, I suspect that I would allow *enmity* to be negatively relevant in such a case … So what we should decide about such cases is rather unclear, or at any rate, the right thing to do about them is not easily compressible into a neat verbal formula – it is likely to be a matter of intuitive judgement, and of what philosophers sometimes call *phronesis* (Aristotle's term for it) or tacit knowledge (cp. Chapter 13). But what these cases do make very clear is that roles overlap, and don't have precise edges. Neither then do the moral standards generated by roles.

As soon as we start thinking about the philosophy of friendship, we face lots of tricky questions like these. If you want quickfire answers to as many as possible of them, then feel free turn at once to Chapter 18, which is a kind of philosophical supermarket-trolley dash that seeks to pile up as many snappy answers to as many snappy questions as quickly as I can.

Some people read philosophy for its answers, others for its questions. Some of us enjoy the journey as well as the destination, and may even not mind if we don't actually reach any destination, any particular answers.

> Philosophy is to be studied, not for the sake of any definite answers to its questions, since no definite answers can, as a rule, be known to be true, but rather for the sake of the questions themselves; because these questions enlarge our conception of what is possible, enrich our intellectual imagination and diminish the dogmatic assurance which closes the mind against speculation. (Russell 1912, final chapter, n. p.)

Maybe what we want is not (or not just) a grab-bag of snappy answers to some philosophical questions about friendship like Chapter 18's, but a more reflective and in-depth exploration of these questions, which links them with all sorts of nearby questions. If that is you, then stay on this page, because that is what the rest of this book supplies.

It's also, on the whole, a better representation of how it is with philosophy. 'Philosophy is a seamless garment', as one of my first and most intimidating philosophy tutors used to say. In philosophy one thing leads to another, and the interconnections are manifold and sometimes surprising. This is partly why good answers to philosophical questions aren't easy to come by: what we say about one question affects what we say about lots of others. This is a book on the philosophy (and the ethics) of friendship. But it is also, and thereby, a book on philosophy and ethics in general, because we can't think about any one ethical or philosophical issue without integrating it into a broader network of other issues.

Nor is there just one correct result for the philosophy of friendship. Despite the attempts of many system-builders to identify and construct one uniquely true theoretical structure, there isn't just one best way of representing any of the subject matter of philosophy. There is no grasping the whole of the truth about philosophy in one single God's-eye view. The nearest any of us can ever get to that kind of synoptic vision is not at all close. It is a particular, accidental, incidental, untidy journey *through* the terrain, undertaken at a particular time, with particular aims and preconceptions, by a particular explorer: in this case, myself.

Two philosophers who will (as it were) keep us company throughout this book, and who always understood this untidiness of philosophy very well – though in their different ways, they both fought against it – are Plato (427–347 BC) and Ludwig Wittgenstein (1889–1951). Plato was (or so we're told) a playwright before Socrates (469–399 BC) converted him to philosophy, and his dramatic artistry is nearly always evident in his work. Philosophy in Plato's dialogues is exactly what I have just described – an untidy journey undertaken by particular people in a particular time and place.

Of course, one of the things that Plato is most famous for is his quest for a kind of superhuman and transcendent clarity and perfection in philosophy – 'the realm of the Forms', as the *Phaedrus* calls it. But I say *quest*. Plato may be searching for – and may long to find – a superhuman order of metaphysical revelation, but it isn't obvious that he ever actually finds that order; whenever he talks about it, he talks about it indirectly and in metaphors. Moreover, his writings remain at nearly all times irresistibly human, and this is part of what makes them such a wonderful read. The philosophical inquiries that he portrays in his dialogues are full of immortal longings. But they always start from a conversation between friends, here and now. And quite often they don't get much further than that; they leave us with more questions than they started with. This is how it is for us too when we do philosophy – and this book will deliberately reflect that messy reality.

Wittgenstein too was something else before he became a philosopher: he was an aeronautical engineer. (He was also a soldier in the Austrian Army in the First World War, and a prisoner of war in Italy. At other times in his life he worked as a gardener, a schoolteacher, and an architect. He probably had the talent to be a musician too, though like many musical people he was gripped by a perfectionist puritanism that found fallibility intolerable.) In line with his strong scientific and technological bent, Wittgenstein began his philosophical career not only as a systematiser, but as one of the most ambitious systematisers of all time. In his *Tractatus Logico-Philosophicus* of 1921, Wittgenstein genuinely believed that he *had* found the uniquely true best single way of representing the subject matter of philosophy. But by the time he wrote the Preface to his *Philosophical Investigations* in January 1945, he had – rather against his will – come to see philosophy completely differently:

> The thoughts which I publish in what follows are the precipitate of philosophical investigations which have occupied me for the last sixteen years. They concern

many subjects ... I have written down all these thoughts
as *remarks*, short paragraphs, of which there is
sometimes a fairly long chain about the same subject,
while I sometimes make a sudden change, jumping from
one topic to another ... The essential thing was that the
thoughts should proceed from one subject to another in a
natural order and without breaks.

After several unsuccessful attempts to weld my results
together into such a whole, I realised that I should never
succeed ... And this was, of course, connected with the
very nature of the investigation. For this compels us to
travel over a wide field of thought criss-cross in every
direction. The philosophical remarks in this book are, as
it were, a number of sketches of landscapes which were
made in the course of these long and
involved journeyings. (1951, v)

'Much contemporary analytic philosophy', the
Oxford philosopher of logic Timothy Williamson has
recently complained, 'seems to be written in the tacit hope
of discursively muddling through, uncontrolled by any clear
methodological constraints' (2007, Afterword). Other philosophers, such as the great Canadian philosopher of science
Ian Hacking, have thought that discursively muddling
through is as good as it gets: first we work out 'what works';
only later, if at all, do we try to work out *why* it works. For
my part, I am on Hacking's side here. I do not proceed
without *any* methodological constraints, but I do take to
heart a thought that is central for Hacking, but which
Williamson seems rather to discount: the thought that our
manner in philosophy ought to be dictated by our matter,
and not the other way around.

The philosophy of friendship is an untidy thing, and in this book, encouraged by the examples of Plato and Wittgenstein, I will mostly be quite unapologetic about the untidiness of my study of it. (Though as I say, anyone who still wants something tidier should try Chapter 18.)

However, there are some things that I *would* like to apologise for.

2 Philosophers of Friendship: An Apology

Chapter 1 has raised a whole range of questions about friendship. Of course many of them had already occurred to me anyway, and no doubt to you too. But a lot of these questions came up, or came up again, when I did my preliminary reading around for this book in the extant philosophical literature on friendship. This goes back a very long way historically, and even today it is still growing alarmingly rapidly.

Anyone who trawls like this through the philosophy of friendship literature will soon notice that philosophers' answers to questions like the ones raised in Chapter 1 – brilliant though they often are – have often also been decidedly po-faced, pompous, out of touch, and (not to put too fine point on it) downright silly. Po-faced, in fact, to the extent that I could hardly blame those possible potential readers who come across this little book of mine in some bookshop (maybe, dear reader, that's just where you are right now) and who ask themselves, 'A philosopher "looks at friendship"? Should a philosopher do that, though? *Another* one? Haven't philosophers made quite enough of a mess in this area already? Isn't their catalogue of silliness full enough yet?'

As we have already seen, philosophers have a bad habit of droning on solemnly about 'the Friendship of Virtue' – portentous capitals intended. Aristotle and many Stoics drone on about this, at least if you translate them unsympathetically. Aristotle seems to hold not only that friendship is possible just between good men, but also that, since friendship is naturally of 'like for like', the limiting case of friendship would be of two pretty well identical people – or it would be a perfect God's contemplative love for himself. (Aristotle's God is not easily describable as 'personal', given that he is almost completely unlike any actual human being – except for his pangalactic self-absorption.) Aristotle's remark that 'A friend is another self' (Aphorism 4 in the Prelude to this book) has a deceptively down-home, calendar-maxim look to it, but there is quite a lot of very peculiar thinking packed into the remark.

Another portentous and overblown thing philosophers tend to do about friendship, which comes with further intentional capitals, is that they go on about 'reverence for Reason As Such as revealed in the other's nature': so Immanuel Kant, in *Groundwork for the Metaphysics of Morals* ([1797] 2017). Or again, if they're theists, philosophers are prone to talk about friends 'seeing the image of God in each other' or the like. Wordsworth sometimes does this, often with more than a dash of the most remarkable and (by our standards) sexist condescension:

> Dear child! dear Girl! that walkest with me here,
> If thou appear untouched by solemn thought,
> Thy nature is not therefore less divine:
> Thou liest in Abraham's bosom all the year;
> And worshipp'st at the Temple's inner shrine,
> God being with thee when we know it not.

Another specimen of philosophical high-mindedness that we have already seen is Cicero's claim (in Aphorism 5) that 'Friendship can exist only between good men'. It's not that there is nothing right about this (at least if we amend *men* to *people*). At least to some degree, people *do* need to be good people to engage in friendship. What we look for in a friend may not be that they be male, still less that they be a po-faced, sententious prig. But it is things like kindness, trustworthiness, loyalty, and honesty. (And common sense.) And these are characteristics of good people, not of bad ones. No one wants to be friends with a cruel, treacherous, disloyal, lying egotist. Not actually *friends* with them, as opposed, conceivably, to thinking it politic or advantageous to show them friendliness. Or if we did want to be friends with someone like that, it would presumably have to be because they have some other redeeming qualities, like that swash-buckling pirate of the Caribbean, Captain Jack Sparrow.

So Cicero's claim that friendship requires goodness of character doesn't seem entirely off the mark. And yet – there's that air of po-facedness again. Even when they are saying something with a grain of truth in it, such po-facedness is everywhere among the philosophers, both past and present, who write about friendship. Take Plato (my favourite philosopher), saying that what we love in our friends is what they reveal to us of the Form of the Good (*Symposium* 210e). Or Montaigne (whom I both like and admire), claiming that it is impossible to have more than one friend at a time (1580). Or Nietzsche (another favourite of mine – he's always entertaining, anyway), who says that a friend should be 'an anticipation of the *Uebermensch*' (1883–1885, para. 62). Or again, we might consider an entire school of philosophers, the utilitarians, whom I must confess

I mostly find it very difficult to love – though there are clear exceptions in the case of some of my oldest friends, and also in the case of John Stuart Mill himself. (And the less utilitarian Mill is, for example in *On Liberty* (1859), the more I like him.) For utilitarians, the most real and basic point of my doing anything is always to optimise: to maximise the good, to do the very best thing in (and for) the entire universe that's available to me. So my friendships are only good when, and insofar as, they help me towards this dizzyingly ambitious and cosmically impersonal objective. And even when they do that, they are always and necessarily under scrutiny: I have to *keep checking* that my friendships are universally optimific. We might reasonably wonder whether someone who has to keep checking *this* is psychologically capable of friendship at all.

For all the profound differences between utilitarianism and Kantianism, we might have a similar worry about Kant's approach to friendship. Utilitarianism tends to turn any friendship into just another way of maximising utility (or failing to), and any friend into just another receptacle in which such utility can be realised (or not). Kantianism tends to turn any friendship into just another arena in which to do our rational Duty (or fail to), and any friend into just another representative of Pure Reason (or not). Some Kantians, for example my friend the eminent American philosopher David Velleman (1999), actually say fairly explicitly that loving a person is loving the Rational Will in them. Both approaches to friendship seem to me a very long way from reality.

The utilitarian approach is also a deeply isolating approach. Kantianism does not share *this* fault, because right at the very basis of Kantianism is the idea of acting for 'a Kingdom of Ends'. A complete understanding of what 'a Kingdom of Ends' might be is not easily attained, but whatever else it means, it clearly involves the idea that all my action is always *inter*action, involving and presupposing the reality of others like myself, and logically committing me to cooperation and coordination with them. And this not merely for the reason that a utilitarian might give – that cooperation and coordination are efficient ways for me to maximise – but for the more fundamental reason that, for Kant, rationality itself is a public and shared possession: in his view, *my being rational* entails, and is entailed by, *our being rational together.* So for Kantians, rational cooperation is not merely instrumentally useful, as it (usually) is for utilitarians; it is itself rationally required.

By contrast, utilitarianism is from its beginning a solitary creed. The basic utilitarian idea can be summed up in a deceptively simple and harmless-looking formula that we get in the work of Derek Parfit: 'There is one ultimate moral aim: that outcomes be as good as possible' (1984, 24). As I say, this sounds innocuous enough. But it is a one-line statement of a philosophical anthropology, a picture of what being a human is all about, that is, I think, profoundly and perniciously false. It is also, paradoxically, completely inimical to the existence of some of the best outcomes there are, including some of the most valuable forms of friendship.

For the utilitarian there is the world, and me the agent, and my mandatory project of improving that world, and that, at bottom, is it. But this turns each of us into a godlike figure who, in everything I do, is at work upon the entire world like Blake's creator God, as it were from the outside; it makes each of us a lonely leverer of utility, trying (all on his or her own) to bring about Maximum Good in the world.

And if we are 'long-termists', like some utilitarians who have recently been much in the news, such as William MacAskill, our efforts must be directed not even merely to the whole of the present world, but instead to some unimaginably distant future worlds where far greater utility will be available for realisation than is now. Previous versions of utilitarianism have usually boiled down to the obviously absurd requirement that each of us should aim (directly or otherwise) at global universal good. Under the name long-termism, utilitarianism's latest and most currently fashionable version now adds to this familiar absurdity the fresh absurdity that each of us should aim at effectively eternal universal good. And aim at it by *whatever means necessary*, even if that included coercion, mind-control, eugenics, forced pregnancy, the replacement of all non-human life by human life on the grounds that humans are more effective and capacious utility-receptacles, or indeed the replacement of all human life by transhuman life on the same grounds.

> In general, population ethics generates an unhealthy interest in other people's reproductive choices. And so, it is no surprise that population ethics is repeatedly entangled in eugenics and race science. And folk who are attracted to this topic tend to take pride in their own steadfast ability to look cold facts into the eyes and their capacity for plain speaking. MacAskill himself is a lot

more cautious, and treats such topics in terms of 'fitness landscapes' and [organismal] and cultural 'traits'.

The key issue is, of course, how MacAskill proposes to achieve the dominance of certain traits. (Schliesser 2023, n.p.)

Like a player trapped in a one-player video game, I am, on the utilitarian picture, the solitary hero of a kind of solipsistic nightmare. And my friends are, for me, simply another way among others for me to assay the titanic task of worldwide (and history-wide) utility-maximisation; similarly as I am, for each of them, simply another way for them to attempt it. It's a pretty bleak tale when you think about it: godlike isolation, without the ambrosia. It's also a pretty barmy picture. Life just isn't like that.

It is a familiar enough criticism of very many versions of utilitarianism that, by the time we get to the theory's workings-out in practice, we seem to be in headlong flight from human reality. We should not miss the deeper point that this flight from the real world is built into utilitarianism from the foundations. But utilitarianism is, unfortunately, a very influential moral theory, and it has spread its influence into all sorts of philosophical debates. For example, one recent debate in ethics that I have contributed to myself is often labelled 'The problem of partiality' (Chappell 2009). Here partiality is something we have already come across, in discussing (early in Chapter 1) the question of whether friendship is a role that we ought to keep or abolish. Partiality is the idea that we are sometimes obliged, or permitted, to act in ways that are not straightforward maximising of the good, because they involve favouring our nearest and dearest. But the idea of acting in those 'partial' ways is surely entirely *un*problematic, unless we start from the utilitarian assumption that our default activity is (or should be) maximising the good. Without that assumption, we are unlikely to call behaviour that doesn't fit the utilitarian default *partiality*, and we are equally unlikely to see such behaviour as a *problem*. Here as elsewhere, the way a philosophical debate develops is often crucially determined by how it is set up in the first place. The way 'the problem of partiality' is usually set up, and the very name that is usually given to it, plays a crucial rhetorical role in driving our thought in a utilitarian direction – which is to say, towards idealisation and the fantasies of rationalism.

For another philosophical fugitive from reality, how about Ralph Waldo Emerson, saying that friendship 'demands a religious treatment'? Emerson is an interesting and sometimes remarkable thinker, but he has an unfortunate tendency to write high-faluting sententious mush. And this tendency comes right out when he talks about friendship:

> It is thought a disgrace to love unrequited. But the great will see that true love cannot be unrequited. True love transcends the unworthy object, and dwells and broods on the eternal, and when the poor interposed mask crumbles, it is not sad, but feels rid of so much earth, and feels its independency the surer ... The essence of friendship is entireness, a total magnanimity and trust. It must not surmise or provide for infirmity. It treats its object as a god, that it may deify both. (Emerson n.d.)

When we read such effusions as this, it is easy to wonder how much fun Emerson can have been at parties, or what his own friends made of this sort of high-minded absurdity. Such remarks may well prompt the question whether Emerson – or quite a few other philosophers – ever actually had any friends themselves. Well, presumably: despite occasional appearances, philosophers are human beings, and most human beings have experienced a friendship. But this just deepens our sense of cognitive dissonance about these philosophers, when we contrast what their biographers tell us of their lives as human beings with what their own books tell us about their theories as philosophers.

A lot of what philosophers have said about friendship is not just po-faced but, to put it bluntly, airy-fairy nonsense. A lot of it is deeply unrealistic, inhumane, and indeed inhuman. So perhaps the most promising beginning that I can offer you is simply an apology for all the po-faced Martian codswallop and pompous cant that we philosophers have all too often talked about friendship. Partly perhaps as a result of my own exasperation – on my recent read-through of the literature of the philosophy of friendship – with at least some of it, I will spend quite a lot of this book pushing back against a lot of what other philosophers have said. With any luck my expostulations will not come across as mere contrarianism, curmudgeonliness, or professional bitching, but will strike a chord with readers, and help us all towards a less hoity-toity and more realistic philosophical appreciation of what friendship is (and isn't), and what friendship can give us (and most certainly won't). At any rate I can promise that I will at least try, in this short book, to do a little better; to talk a little better than nonsense.

A little better? Well, we'll see.

3   Why I Don't Start with a Formal Definition of Friendship

T here is another important mistake that it is traditional for us philosophers to start our inquiries with, that I want to attack head on and straight away. This is an obvious falsehood that often blocks our inquiries altogether, namely the idea that you can't get anywhere in philosophical inquiry unless you start with a formal, explicit, and watertight definition. No such definition is available in most of the cases that philosophy is interested in. And that includes our topic here, friendship. This is why I have got two chapters into the topic and counting, and I still haven't offered any formal definition of friendship. I won't be offering a definition any later, either – not even in the Q & A session in Chapter 18 – except in a loose and informal way.

Fortunately, this traditional falsehood has never been universally embraced in philosophy. But it has always had a certain popularity and intellectual prestige. Philosophers can rarely resist a chance to look like they are achieving maximum clarity, no doubt because most of the questions that they are professionally concerned with are perennially shrouded in maximum obscurity. (Compare Bertrand Russell's remarks in Chapter 1.)

The false doctrine of the indispensable primacy of formal definitions takes us back again to Plato, because it is an aspect of what is usually known as the *Socratic method*.

(There are other aspects to the Socratic method, but this is one central feature of it.) Socrates often found his inquiries stymied by his own insistence on definitions – sometimes to the point where he professed himself completely stuck, or confessed that he ended the discussion with less knowledge (or apparent knowledge) than he had started it with.

Socrates plays a starring role in most of the philosophical dialogues written by his greatest pupil Plato – dialogues which are studies in philosophy but also, very strikingly, studies of friendships too. Especially in Plato's earlier dialogues, Socrates tries repeatedly to get the friends or other acquaintances whom he is arguing with to define a whole range of usually ethical concepts, often the names of virtues. So he investigates self-control in the *Charmides*, courage in the *Laches*, virtue itself in the *Meno* and the *Protagoras*, justice in *Republic* Book 1, love in the *Symposium*, wisdom/knowledge in the *Theaetetus* – and friendship in the *Lysis*. Though there are plenty of variations, the recurring pattern in these dialogues is that Socrates' interlocutors try to define the target concept, but their efforts fall apart under Socrates' inquisition. Socrates then triumphantly concludes that they don't know even the first thing about the concept they're inquiring into.

Of course, in any inquiry a useful initial question is 'What are we actually talking about?', to help us get any distracting ambiguities out of the way. And there are some inquiries where we should certainly start out not just from this sort of rough indication of topic but from formal definitions, inquiries where starting from the right definition will do most of the conceptual leg-work for us, if we just think about it. The most obvious inquiry like that is geometry – which, not coincidentally, was Plato's favourite science. Greeks of Plato's time tended to think of geometry as, basically, the science of circles and triangles; it was the area of mathematics in which the ancient Greeks made the most progress, impeded as they were by their clunky numbering system, which was rather like the Roman numerals.

The most famous geometrician of all time was the Alexandrian Greek Euclid (325–265 BC), who was born about twenty years after Plato died. Euclid's procedure was to start by laying down definitions and axioms, then put them together to arrive at the theorems that followed logically from them. Theorems are timeless, certain, and provable truths, which are true just in virtue of what triangles timelessly and universally are, and which apply, not just to *these triangles here in front of us*, but to any possible triangle anywhere ever. So wherever we can apply the Euclidean method, we can get timeless, certain, and logically provable knowledge.

Like many later philosophers – Gottfried Wilhelm Leibniz, Baruch de Spinoza, Jeremy Bentham, Gottlob Frege, even Bertrand Russell – Plato's ambition was, if possible, to do *all* inquiry by something like a geometrical method. In Plato's *Meno*, a geometrical proof that is a corollary of Pythagoras' theorem is both figuratively and literally central to the dialogue, and the challenge is to see if the kind of reasoning involved in that proof can be applied more generally, to the definition of virtue. In Plato's *Theaetetus*, the first speaker is even (albeit coincidentally) called Euclid. Early on in the discussion, Theaetetus himself – the brilliant young mathematician after whom the dialogue is named – rather proudly explains to Socrates how he and his companions have been investigating cube roots and square roots using two-dimensional and three-dimensional figures. So Socrates challenges Theaetetus to apply the same level of rigour to the question that he wants answered, 'What is knowledge?' (*Theaetetus* 148d): 'Take your answer about the square roots and the cube roots as a model, and just as you found a way to put all of them in one single class, though they were many, try to capture all the many forms of knowledge in one single definition.'

Many philosophers past and present have followed out their own impulse to systematise, often with a quite unwarranted confidence in the possibility of such systematisations in philosophy. Like most of those systematisers, Meno and Theaetetus both fail. Neither of them can find a definition of the concepts that they're inquiring into (virtue and knowledge respectively) that can play a foundational role in philosophical inquiry in anything like the way that definitions play a foundational role in geometry. But this failure on the part of *Plato's characters* is not a failure on *Plato*'s part. Plato is exploring the limitations of the geometrical method, and of philosophical systematisation more generally, and he is perfectly well aware of it when his inquiry hits those limits.

One thing that all good philosophers understand is that there is often more to be learned from our failures than our successes. Plato is one of the best philosophers who ever lived, and it is no accident that he presents, in so many of his dialogues, a line of philosophical argument that doesn't work out. We want to know things, and to know them with the kind of certainty and cogency that Pythagorean or

Euclidean geometry bestows on knowledge. But there are some concepts that we can't define in the formal, explicit, and watertight way that we can define the concepts of geometry. One lesson that we might draw from Plato's writings is that this is true of most of the concepts that are central to philosophy. It is true of virtue and knowledge. And it is also true of friendship. As I said at the end of Chapter 1, our method should be shaped to fit our material, and not the other way around.

There are two significant questions that arise from this failed attempt to find rigorous definitions for such key philosophical concepts as knowledge, virtue, and friendship. Both questions are often especially audible in Plato's own middle to late writings, for example in the *Republic*, the *Sophist*, the *Statesman*, and the *Philebus*. The first question is: 'Why the *difference* between geometrical and philosophical inquiries?'; the second is: 'Can philosophical inquiries find a *substitute* for the rigour of formal definition that is seen in geometry?' For answers to these questions, we may turn to two figures much closer to us in the history of philosophy: Friedrich Nietzsche (1844–1900) and Ludwig Wittgenstein (1889–1951).

On 'Why the difference?': in his 1887 polemic *On the Genealogy of Morals*, Nietzsche writes: 'All concepts in which a whole process is semiotically comprehended elude definition; only something that has no history can be defined' ([1887] 2013, 2.13). To understand what a triangle is, is to understand something that has no history. A triangle is what it is, irrespective of how people have thought or felt about triangles down the ages. But how, historically, people have thought and felt about knowledge, and virtue, and friendship, and what if anything they want to do with those concepts in their own lives, is crucial to what these three things are.

Philosophy tends to focus on timeless abstractions, and to ask definitional questions about them that presuppose that, once we know what X is, we know what X is *at any time or place*. But friendship is most certainly something that has a history. As soon as we think about some of the best-known examples of friendship in literature – about Homer in contrast to Jane Austen, or Shakespeare in contrast to Dickens in contrast to *Tom Brown's Schooldays* (Hughes 1857), to mention five examples that we shall come to – we see the differences between what friendship is or was in the different social worlds of these five authors, and so with many others. It could not be more obvious that what friendship is, and is taken to involve, has varied from one era to another, and from one place or milieu to another too: friendship has a geography as well as a history. This diversity is of great interest in its own right; these differences are not a problem to any investigator who approaches the topic of friendship in the right spirit. But philosophers are naturally tempted to treat the differences as incidental 'clothing' or 'presentation' of one and the same essential thing – friendship – so that we need to strip these superficialities away to get at the real thing, the historically unchangeable underlying essence of friendship. This 'striptease' approach is not the right way to approach the topic of friendship – nor indeed most other topics in philosophy.

Part of what I am criticising here is a certain kind of tunnel vision about friendship: an insistence that it must have a particular nature that we can specify easily in terms that we already understand. Here as elsewhere, my watchword is 'Broaden your minds'. There are all kinds of things that friendship might be, and our society (more exactly our society up to this point) has no particular monopoly on the notion, and no special authority to describe it (or, to anticipate what's coming next, to prescribe about it). To think that we know already exactly what friendship is and can only be involves a certain kind of cultural arrogance – and a quite unnecessary constraint on our moral imaginations.

In ethics, moreover, we see a certain kind of *observer interference.* In physics there are famously bizarre exceptional cases (such as the 'twin-slit experiment') where just to observe the phenomena is itself to affect them. In ethics too there are cases where observation of the phenomena itself makes a difference to those phenomena. But in ethics, in contrast to physics, such cases are not exceptional, but the norm. In ethics it happens all the time that we have to deal with cases where just to talk about how things are is itself to make a difference to how things are. In ethics, *to describe is to prescribe*; to represent is already to intervene.

Iris Murdoch sums up what I have in mind here when she writes that 'Man is a creature who makes pictures of himself, and then comes to resemble the picture' (1999, 75). Her remark is very readily applicable to the philosophy of friendship. In writing this book about friendship I am, naturally, trying to give a picture of friendship, trying to say how things are with friendship. But saying how things are with friendship is not like saying how things are with the temperature of a test-tube or the reciprocal of pi. If we are doing philosophy, and not just a sociological survey, then to say how things *are* with friendship is necessarily to say how things *should be* with friendship. It is to make a further move in a continuing debate about what friendship *ought to be for us*: either a move that makes a more or less revealing proposal about how to see friendship in a new way – or a move that implicitly directs us to 'keep things as they were'. So if we *succeed* in saying how things are with friendship, then necessarily we *change* how things are with friendship. This phenomenon of observer interference makes the subject matter of ethics, including topics like friendship, somewhat elusive, though not – let us hope – impossibly so.

We come back here to something that I mentioned in Chapter 1: thick ethical concepts. It is characteristic and usual for them to have histories. And these histories can become, or intersect with, individual people's ethical biographies, the development of their moral outlook over time. For a key part of such outlooks will be what thick ethical concepts any individual accepts or rejects, and why.

So, for example, Oscar Wilde famously said (at his second trial, 3 April 1895) that '"Blasphemous" is not a word of mine.' Wilde meant that BLASPHEMY was a thick concept that he rejected, that he had no place for it in his ethical understanding of himself and others. He could not have said, in parallel with this, that '"Triangular" is not a word of mine.' The concept of a triangle is not (in any obvious way) an ethical concept, or a thick concept, or a concept with a history. It is not part of anyone's self-understanding, and is not up for acceptance or rejection by anyone – not even by a decidedly Nietzschean spirit like Wilde. The idea of the triangle is not constituted at all, not even partially, by people's or societies' expectations or wishes or aspirations or self-consciousness – by the place that people would like triangles to have in their lives. But the ideas of virtue and friendship *are* constituted, in part, by the place that these concepts have in societies' and individuals' changing and historically various conceptions of themselves. To put it rather as it might have been put by Nietzsche's great adversary G. W. F. Hegel (1770–1831), the whole point of concepts like TRIANGLE is that they are not in the least entangled with our own historically conditioned self-consciousness. And the whole point of concepts like FRIENDSHIP is that they *are* entangled with our history and our self-awareness. For such concepts, describing and prescribing are closely connected: laying out what we think friendship *is* is very close to laying out what we think friendship *should be*. It isn't, in any very obvious way, like that with triangles.

So much for the first question identified above, why the difference of role between definition in science and in cases like friendship. As for the other question, 'Can philosophy find a *substitute* for geometry's rigorous formal definitions?': my answer is 'Yes'. We may not be able to define 'friend' or 'friendship' with the same rigorous, counter-example-free exactitude with which we can define 'triangle' or 'circle'. But never mind. We can still use a form of words to give a *rough* indication of what friendship is.

If I was challenged to do this, I'd say that friendship is *benevolent companionship over time*. Such a loose definition faces objections like the fact that friends can be thoroughly malicious (so not benevolent), or distant (so not companions), or very brief (so not over time). But as I say, this rough indication of the nature of friendship is not meant to be invincibly counter-example-proof. My provisional definition can coexist with these objections.

We might also give a rough indication of the nature of friendship rather in the way that a dictionary does. The first dictionary I pick off the shelf is the *Shorter Oxford English Dictionary* of 1933, and this is how it defines 'friend':

> 1/ 'One joined to another in mutual benevolence and intimacy' (J) [= Johnson; cp. Aphorism 12]. Not ordinarily used of lovers or relatives. 2/ Applied loosely, e.g. to a mere acquaintance. 3/ A kinsman or near relation. 4/ A lover or paramour of either sex. 5/ One who wishes (another, a cause, etc.) well; a sympathiser, a supporter. 6/ One not an enemy.

'Not ordinarily', 'applied loosely': this definition itself admits that it isn't watertight, that it isn't even trying to be completely resistant to all possible counter-examples. (Here is one obvious counter-example to the first part of this definition: I have plenty of people who I would say are my friends, but with whom I am certainly not *intimate*. Nor are we 'joined to one another', as it were like conjoined twins. With most of my friendships, including my close ones, the very idea has an air of absurdity to it.) The dictionary definition also falls short of Plato's geometrical requirements because it is something like a *list*: more about lists in a moment. Still, this loose dictionary definition gives us a rough and imprecise idea of what it is to be a friend. If friendship is, as I am arguing, itself a rough and imprecise notion, then not only is this dictionary definition, or my own characterisation of friendship as benevolent companionship over time, all we need by way of a defining formula; it's also true that any greater precision would be spurious.

Another, perhaps slightly offbeat, way of getting clearer about what friendship is, is to ask: What is the *opposite* of friendship? Where a thing has more than one opposite, or a range of contrary states none of which is exactly the opposite of it, that shows some complexity in the thing. And this is certainly true of friendship. In one way, *loneliness* is the opposite of friendship, because friendship answers to our need for companions. But in a second way, *indifference* is the opposite of friendship, because friendship answers to our need for companions who are interested in us. And in a third, *hatred* is of course the opposite of friendship, because friendship answers to our need for companions who are not only interested, but also benevolently interested in us. Maybe friendship has other opposites or contrary states besides loneliness, indifference, and hatred, but in a small way, it is already interesting and illuminating that it has all three of these.

4   Examples of Friendship

T alk of lists brings us to another way of indicating what friendship is without formally defining it. This begins from a complaint that Wittgenstein makes about the Socratic method. Wittgenstein is not much given to engagement with other philosophers; especially in his later works, he often sounds like a man who is arguing mainly with himself. But in the 1930s notebooks, unpublished in his lifetime, that we now call *The Blue and Brown Books*, he offers this criticism of the Socratic method:

> The idea that in order to get clear about the meaning of a general term one had to find the common element in all its applications has shackled philosophical investigation; for it has not only led to no result, but also made the philosopher dismiss the concrete cases, which alone could have helped him to understand the usage of the general term. When Socrates asks the question, 'What is knowledge?', he does not regard it even as a *preliminary* answer to enumerate cases of knowledge. (1958, 20)

Wittgenstein is picking up on the fact that what Theaetetus offers as his first and preliminary answer to Socrates' question is, precisely, an enumeration of cases of knowledge. Here is Theaetetus' list:

> I think the things that one might learn from my tutor Theodorus are kinds of knowledge: geometry, and his

> other areas of study. Also cobbling and the other manual
> labourers' crafts. All of these are nothing other than
> knowledge; each of these is nothing other than a kind
> of knowledge. (Plato, *Theaetetus* 146c–d)

Wittgenstein might equally have cited the *Meno*, where Socrates challenges Meno to define virtue, and Meno responds with another list – this time of examples of virtue:

> *Meno.* It's not hard to say what virtue is. If you want the
> virtue of a man first, that's easy. A man's virtue is to be
> man enough to run his city's affairs, and to run them so
> as to benefit his friends and harm his enemies – and
> make sure that no such harm ever comes to himself.
> Then if you want a woman's virtue, that's not hard to
> state either. What she has to do is keep house well,
> looking after the property and obeying her husband.
> A child's virtue is another thing, and it is different again
> depending on whether we mean a boy's virtue or a girl's.
> And there is a specific virtue for an old man, with further
> differences depending on whether he is a free old man or
> a slave. There are any number of other varieties of virtue
> too. So it's hardly a problem, Socrates, to say what the
> definition of virtue is. There is a specific virtue for each
> sort of activity and age, for each of us, in whatever we do.
> And likewise, I suppose, for vice. (Plato, *Meno* 71e–72d)

Socrates bats away both these answers in the *Theaetetus* and *Meno* respectively, and in such similar words that many commentators, including me (Chappell 2003, 36), have suggested that the *Theaetetus* passage deliberately echoes the *Meno*:

> I do seem to be having the most remarkable luck today, Meno. I was only after *one* virtue, but to judge by your description, I have found a whole swarm. (*Meno* 72d)

> A noble answer, Theaetetus. A generous one, too: you were asked for one thing and you give us lots of things, you were asked for something simple and you give us the whole gamut. (*Theaetetus* 146d)

Socrates is dismissive about Meno's and Theaetetus' catalogues of examples of virtue and knowledge. But if Nietzsche is right that virtue and knowledge are historically conditioned concepts, we should dismiss Socrates' dismissiveness. As Wittgenstein says, these lists of examples show us in concrete and particular terms what virtue and knowledge are – which partly means, what virtue and knowledge have been in history.

Specifically to their own place in history, Meno's and Theaetetus' lists give us lots of important information about how the Greeks of Plato's time ordinarily thought about knowledge and virtue. For example, Theaetetus' list shows clearly that they intuitively thought that knowledge was exemplified not only by precise studies like geometry, but also by practical endeavours like handiwork. As for Meno's list, it is virtually a potted sociology. Meno is telling us what counts as being a good person in the various social roles that Athenians typically occupied in Plato's time. In the process he gives us some valuable and fascinating insights into what those social roles actually were.

So it is rather unfair of Socrates to criticise Meno's account of virtue for its shapeless multiplicity (*Meno* 72b ff.), its lack of clear essential unity, when in fact Meno's aim is to demonstrate exactly that multiplicity. Meno's point – presumably; one can only speculate, because Socrates never gives the point anything like a fair hearing – is that virtue is *one* thing that occurs in multiple ways in multiple contexts, and that understanding it is largely a matter of tracing it through these modulations and applications. (So also with Protagoras' account of virtue: Plato, *Protagoras* 329b–333b.)

Likewise, I suggest, with friendship. On its normal and most natural conception among the ancient Greeks, friendship – *philia* – is naturally patient of a very similar style of account to Meno's of virtue. *Philia* too is one thing, but crops up in different modulations in different contexts. Thus *philia* to parents, children, or siblings is family affection; *philia* to a spouse or lover is sexual or romantic love; *philia* to a peer in age and status is friendship. And relationships with peers can be further subdivided, perhaps, depending on the specificities of social structure. (Maybe along the lines that Aristotle suggests – but more about that in Chapter 9.)

So with friendship as with virtue and knowledge, a list of examples of friendship will be highly useful. How plausible we find any given general philosophical claim or argument typically depends on which range of specific examples we have in the back of our minds when we consider it. I have made this point elsewhere, in my book *Epiphanies* (Chappell 2022b, ch. 1, sect. 2), and Iris Murdoch makes it too, in an essay titled 'Vision and Choice in Morality':

> It is especially important to attend to the initial delineation of the field of study ... A narrow or partial

selection of phenomena may suggest certain particular techniques which will in turn seem to lend support to that particular selection; and then a circle is formed out of which it may be hard to break. It is therefore advisable to return frequently to an initial survey of 'the moral' so as to consider, in the light of a primary apprehension of what morality is, what our technical devices actually do for us. (1999, 33)

Many otherwise incomprehensible disagreements in philosophy apparently depend on precisely this sort of difference between our background example-sets. I say that something is good, you say that it is bad, because each of us is, inside her own head, reacting to a different range of examples from her own experiential back-catalogue. In order to understand adequately what things are, not just by abstract knowledge of a verbal definition but by experiential knowledge – first- or second-hand – we need to have a good range of examples before us, and to be explicitly aware that it is *that* range of examples that is driving our intuitions and responses.

If you want to get a clear idea what friendship is, forget about *definitions* of friendship (at least in any watertight formal sense). Think instead – as we have in fact been doing since the very beginning of this book – about *examples* of friendship. Who are your friends, and why do you count them as friends? Who is your best friend? Which people that you know are only marginal cases of friends for you, and *why* are they only marginal? What do you expect from someone whom you call a friend, and what do you expect them to expect from you? Do you pick friends because they are good people, or because you simply like them – or a bit of both? Do you pick friends because they are similar to you ('Birds of a feather' again), or different ('Opposites attract') – or a bit of both? What do you think someone would have to be like to be what you would call a *perfect* friend – or anywhere near perfect?

Also: which are your favourite books or films (or games, or radio dramas, or graphic novels, or whatever) that depict a friendship, and why are they your favourites? Here, in case it helps, are some of *my* favourite fictional friendships. Quite a few of them have already come up in this discussion, and throughout this book I will continue to assemble more examples of friendship, both from fiction and from real-world history:

> Thelma and Louise, in *Thelma and Louise*
> Jane Bennet and Lizzy Bennet, in *Pride and Prejudice*
> Shrek and Donkey, in *Shrek*
> Eugene Wrayburn and Mortimer Lightwood, in *Our Mutual Friend*
> Algernon and Jack, in *The Importance of Being Earnest*
> Ratty and Mole, in *The Wind in the Willows*
> Virgil and Dante, in *The Inferno*
> David Tennant and Michael Sheen, in *Staged*
>
> Sherlock Holmes and John Watson, both as they appear in Arthur Conan Doyle's original *Sherlock Holmes* books and as played by Benedict Cumberbatch and Martin Freeman in the more recent TV drama series *Sherlock*.

Obviously, different cases of friendship differ from each other. And obviously, you will have your own ideas about which are your favourite fictional friends; for instance, you might be a fan of *Friends*. (Unlike me; I've never seen it.) Even more obviously, your real-life friends are one set of people, and my real-life friends are another set, and it's more than likely that we don't have any mutuals.

That's all fine. The point is just for each of us to think about friendship with a clear set of examples before our minds: a set of examples of friendship that we know about, that resonates and makes sense for us, and brings alive for us the questions that we are considering about friendship. And the point is for each of us to be self-aware enough to understand which examples of friendship it is that tend to drive our own intuitions, and to notice, as above, that other people's intuitions about friendship may well differ from ours, *simply because* they are working with different examples of friendship.

5   Beginning the Natural History of Friendship

So we should begin the philosophy of friendship not with a formal, logically watertight definition, but rather with a rough definition of friendship, such as my own characterisation of friendship as benevolent companionship over time, or such as the dictionary definition that I quote in Chapter 3. We can also base our reflections on the question 'What is opposite to friendship?', and on an explicit and conscious list of examples of friendship. And it's all the better if this list *is* explicit and conscious, because our thoughts about friendship almost certainly will be guided by our own experiences of friendship whether we realise it or not, so we will be using *some* list of examples either consciously or unconsciously; consciously is preferable.

We can use a third help too: a help which is already suggested by lists like Meno's of kinds of virtue, and Theaetetus' of kinds of knowledge. Those lists, as I commented above, are rich resources for thinking about *the place in human life*, both individual and social, of virtue and knowledge. Likewise, the most helpful question to ask about friendship may well not be so much 'What is the definition of friendship?' as 'What is the place of friendship in human life?'.

Human beings are a zoological species, and to understand them we need to understand them *as* a zoological species. So to understand friendship, we need to understand how friendship fits into the life of our species. We need to consider friendship as something that has not only a history, a record of different manifestations in different times and places, but also a natural history.

What is a natural history, and what is the natural history of friendship? A natural history is a zoological or biological story, a life-cycle narrative. Such a narrative can be given for any living species that has a life-cycle at all. For example, natural histories can be narrated both for amoebae and for kangaroos. And here, thanks to Wikipedia, are some edited highlights of the natural histories of just those two life forms:

> Amoebae move and feed by using pseudopods, which are bulges of cytoplasm formed by the coordinated action of actin microfilaments pushing out the plasma membrane that surrounds the cell . . . The food sources of amoebae vary. Some amoebae are predatory and live by consuming bacteria and other protists. Some are detritivores and eat dead organic material . . . Amoebae have been found to harvest and grow the bacteria implicated in plague. Amoebae can likewise play host to microscopic organisms that are pathogenic to people and help in spreading such microbes. Recent evidence indicates that several Amoebozoa lineages undergo meiosis. (https://en.wikipedia.org/wiki/Amoeba)

> Groups of kangaroos are called *mobs*, *courts* or *troupes*, which usually have 10 or more kangaroos in them . . . Larger aggregations display high amounts of interactions and complex social structures, comparable to that of ungulates. One common behaviour is nose touching and sniffing, which mostly occurs when an

individual joins a group. The kangaroo performing the sniffing gains much information from smell cues. This behaviour enforces social cohesion without consequent aggression. During mutual sniffing, if one kangaroo is smaller, it will hold its body closer to the ground and its head will quiver, which serves as a possible form of submission ... Most other non-antagonistic behaviour occurs between mothers and their young. Mother and young reinforce their bond through grooming ... Sexual activity of kangaroos consists of consort pairs. (https://en .wikipedia.org/wiki/Kangaroo)

We can tell a natural-history story like these two about any zoological species (or group of species), including kangaroos and amoebae. And human beings are a zoological species. So we can tell a natural-history story about human beings. If we do, how does it go? And where does *friendship* fit into it?

According to modern child psychologists, some at least of the answer looks like this:

LEVEL 0: **Momentary Playmates** (3–7 years): Children at this stage view friends as momentary playmates, and their friendships are all about having fun together. Their friends are kids who are conveniently nearby, and who do the same things they like to do ...

LEVEL 1: **One-Way Assistance** (4–9 years): At this level, children ... define friends as children who do nice things for them ... but they don't really think about what they themselves contribute to the friendship. Children at this level ... may put up with a not-so-nice friend, just so they can have a friend. They also may try to use friendship as a bargaining tool ...

LEVEL 2: Two-Way, Fair Weather Cooperation (6–12 years): These children . . . are very concerned about fairness and reciprocity, but they think about these in a very rigid way . . . They tend to be jealous, and they're very concerned with fitting in by being exactly the same as everyone else. Children at this stage often form small friendship groups [such] as 'secret clubs' which involve elaborate rules and lots of discussion about who is or isn't included as a member . . .

LEVEL 3: Intimate, Mutually Shared Relationships (11–15 years): At this stage, friends help each other solve problems and confide thoughts and feelings that they don't share with anyone else. They know how to compromise, and they do kind things for each other without 'keeping score,' because they genuinely care about each other's happiness. For some children, this is also the 'Joined at the Hip' stage . . .

LEVEL 4: Mature Friendship (12 years to adulthood): At this stage, children place a high value on emotional closeness with friends. They can accept and even appreciate differences between themselves and their friends. Young people who develop mature friendships are not as possessive as they might once have been, so they're less likely to feel threatened if their friends have other relationships. Mature friendship emphasises trust and support and remaining close over time, despite separations. (https://kids-first.com.au/the-5-stages-of-childrens-friendships/)

This popular summary of a whole academic literature of quantitative scientific research in developmental social psychology tells us something important about the natural history of friendship in the human species: about how small children, and then young people, first get socialised into friendship as an idea and a social practice. Much of the summary, no doubt, will strike chords for many of us in the light of our own experience. And no doubt we could extend the summary to cover later parts of life, and get a larger longitudinal picture of how people practise and enjoy – or fail to enjoy – their friendships in the rest of their lifespans.

As the authors of the summary notice, friendships among school-children are often highly competitive affairs – it's not just about friends, it's about *best* friends. And number of friends, too: having as many friends as possible is taken as a key sign of status and success, and no one wants to be the school-child with no friends. So often friendships among small children are pretty intense. As I know from my own parenting experience, ten-year-old girls can get very dramatic indeed about who their friends are and, perhaps even more crucially, aren't (the 'Joined at the Hip' stage, as it is called above); though as girls get older – and as romance and/or marriage appear as alternatives to friendship – they typically get more relaxed about their friendships. Later on in this book I will be arguing that friendship is an unemphatic good; the case of ten-year-old girls reminds me to qualify this by saying that *mature* friendships are *typically* an unemphatic good.

Certainly among those who are socially ambitious, having as many friends as possible continues to be an aim even when they are grown up. But many people become distinctly more introverted as they grow older – more inter-ested in the friends that they already have than in making new friends. I freely admit that this is true of me, and Aristotle implicitly recognises it too: he notes (*Nicomachean Ethics* 1158a1–3) that older people are more prone than the young to the character defect of moroseness, to a lack of friendliness and openness to new possible friends. After all, when you have known most of your main friends for fifty years or more, it is quite unlikely that you will find it equally rewarding to start up a new friendship with someone that you've only just met. And from this there comes a kind of paradox that faces us all in old age. Just at the point where 'the younger generation' are becoming increasingly unrelatable and incomprehensible, just at the point where it seems natural to fall back on those of your own generation who share your own outlook and values and frames of reference, to give up trying to make new friends and just fall back on your old friends – those old friends unfortunately start dying off.

Mortality is not of course the only problem about friendship that old people distinctively face, and Aristotle is certainly right to identify moroseness as one of the main ones. To risk some generalisations (no doubt they have plenty of refreshing exceptions), old people tend to lack the optimism, the flexibility (both physical and psychological), and the energy that are such delightful assets of the young; old people's friendships have had longer than young people's to meet the kind of impasse or sustain the kind of insult that makes it impossible for the friendship to continue. The older we get, the easier it becomes to stay within the ever-shrinking comfort zone of those we haven't fallen out with – or not yet. The older we get, the more we are inclined to stand on our dignity. And so, the older we get, the likelier we are to find ourselves with little company left but our own long grudges. There are few better bits of advice in the Bible than St Paul's in Ephesians 4.26, 'Do not let the sun go down on your anger.' But it takes get-up-and-go to act on this advice, and get-up-and-go is, above all things, what young people typically have, and old people sadly lack.

> Chill on the brow and in the breast
> The frost of years is spread;
> Soon we shall take our endless rest
> With the unfeeling dead.
>
> Insensibly, ere we depart,
> We grow more cold, more kind:
> Age makes a winter in the heart,
> An autumn in the mind.
>
> (John Sparrow, 1981, 16)

No doubt there are some universal elements in this summary 'natural history of friendship among humans'. After all, every human life involves being born, growing up, getting old (if you're lucky), and dying. Still, that summary natural history is highly culturally specific. It is talking about friendship in some particular modern 'Western' societies: Australia in the case of the first bit (the quotation about the stages of friendship among children) and other modern Western societies for the rest of it. We can get an outline natural history of friendship among humans that is true despite these differences between societies, but for a fuller understanding of friendship, we need to take these differences more seriously. For as Aristotle phrased it at the opening of the *Politics* (1253a), 'Man is a social animal', an animal that lives in societies; it is the nature of humanity to have not just a nature but a culture too.

Now humans are not the only animals who have something like a culture. After all, we have just seen a quotation, above, that suggests that there are social groupings among kangaroos. Presumably there aren't social, as opposed to biochemical, groupings among amoebae, but plenty of non-human species besides kangaroos show variation over time and space in shared tropes of behaviour which are not obviously 'hard-wired' into them by evolutionary processes, and which are picked up by imitative learning and reinforced both by their effectiveness and by others' approval or disapproval. For example, some orca populations have distinctive strategies for hunting seals; different whale pods sing different songs; and some groups of crows display problem-solving techniques that other groups of crows do not display.

However, human beings seem fairly clearly *more* various and more sophisticated than most other species in the cultures that they have developed. (In other ways we as a species are far less various; for example, our DNA stock is extremely small compared with most other mammals'.) All this variety and sophistication complicates the natural history of the human species. The tale we have to tell about the natural history of our species can't be purely zoological; it needs to be anthropological and sociological as well. For human cultures and societies differ from each other, both in time and in space. And one of the main ways in which they differ is precisely in their conception of friendship.

Here are some examples of this variety. Chinese society today, including and in particular the business world, is built around the basically Confucian notion of *guanxi*: mutual trust, loyalty, and respect. *Guanxi* is clearly a kind of friendship, but the word literally means 'closed system'. Again, in Chapter 3 I quoted the Oxford English Dictionary (OED) definition of 'friend' on which – according to Oxford academics in the 1930s – the word is 'not ordinarily used of lovers or relatives'. But the nearest ancient Greek equivalent to 'friend' is *philos*, and among the ancient Greeks a person's *philoi* were simply all those she loved (*philei*) – her lovers, her relatives, *and* what we would call her friends. (Sophocles' character Antigone, for example, uses that one word of all of these categories.) Again, in pre-Columbian North America, and among the Scythians and the Huns according to Herodotus (*Histories* 4.70), there was the tradition of blood brothership, of making a lifelong pact of mutual loyalty by a symbolic exchange of a small amount of blood. Or consider the ancient Romans, for whom the hierarchical social relation of patron and client was economically and politically crucial, as it also seems to have been in, for example, the more or less completely feudal societies that Dante and Shakespeare lived in. Again, another crucial tradition that is seen in many different societies is the tradition of guest–host formalities. Many societies have found it important to manage expectations by setting the dangerous and risky business of encountering new and unknown fellow humans within a ritual framework of one sort or another. So in Roman and ancient Greek societies there were elaborate duties involved in being either a host or a guest, and the roles of host and guest both came with religious imperatives and sanctions involved; the Latin word for guest, *hospes*, is also the Latin word for host, and likewise with *xenos* in ancient Greek.

All of these various concepts involve something like a notion of friendship. But they all differ from each other, and they also differ from the kinds of friendship that we find familiar. The instantiations of friendship within any culture will vary over time, and may well vary in quality too. (People might worry, as contemporary Western journalists sometimes do, that there is not enough friendship in their society, or alternatively, though this seems less likely, that there is too much.) Friendship is deeply culturally various; it has a history, indeed different histories in different societies. All this helps to bring out the wisdom in Nietzsche's remark, quoted in Chapter 3, that 'only something that has no history can be defined' ([1887] 2013, 2.13). It is because friendship is situated in time and space in these ways that we cannot make sense of it just with an abstract definition, however formally watertight it may be. To understand friendship properly, we need to understand what friendship has meant to many different people in many different eras of history, and across the spaces of many different countries and societies.

So our task is to understand not just friendship in any narrow sense, but the broader background notion of human sociality in general within which that narrow conception of friendship is situated. It is after all one of the ways in which our society has a particular conception of friendship, that it typically takes friendship to be something narrower than sociality in general. It is possible to see friendship this way – and possible not to. Other societies have often had a broader notion of friendship than ours, as evidenced by the much wider semantic range of the Greek word *philos*. Respecting this kind of point is part of our general duty to respect the variability of friendship over history, and across geography.

We need to keep in mind this obligation to time and space, to recognising and doing justice to the vast historical and geographical variations that there have been in people's conceptions of friendship. But provided we do keep it in mind, there is nothing to prevent us from going further with the natural history of friendship among humans – as we will in Chapter 6.

6 Deepening the Natural Historical Account

At the most basic level of natural history, some creatures simply do not get on well living solitarily, and do much better when they are part of a larger group of some sort. There are species of mammal for which it is natural and normal to live alone (except for breeding and rearing purposes): for example snow leopards, and polar bears, and platypuses, and moose. But such species as lions, and sheep, and gorillas, and sparrows, and dolphins are plainly social species. Elephants and chimps are well known for the clear distress that they show at the loss of a member of their group. Every dog owner knows how a pet dog will go on looking for another pet dog, or for a member of its human family, after they have died. Anyone who wants to keep rabbits is advised by all the experts to make sure that it is indeed *rabbits*, plural, and not just a single rabbit. Even cats, though they often seem to project a sleek air of solitary superiority, are in fact nearly always busy seeking out the company both of humans (especially ones with food and warmth to share) and of other cats (especially ones that they can either fight or fornicate with). For all these kinds of animals, it is obviously and demonstrably true that living together is better than living in isolation. And this seems to be such a general, physiology-level fact that it is almost superfluous to ask *why* they do better in company: they just do, in a whole range of very basic ways.

71

The same basic physiological fact also holds, apparently, of human beings. Whatever else you may think of the anthropology of Genesis, there is a profound truth in the Prelude's second aphorism, Genesis 2.18: 'It is not good for man to be alone.' Friendship, or at least companionship, or even mere company, has clear psychological benefits for us, in a whole range of very basic ways. It is not for nothing that solitary confinement is often seen as a form of psychological torture.

It is typical of philosophers to want to analyse this fact by way of reasons – '*Why* is friendship good for us?', 'What are the specific benefits of friendship?' I will do some of that too, later in this chapter and elsewhere. But the first thing that I want to point out is the extent to which the goodness of friendship is just a fact about our natural history that, we might say, goes deeper than any reasons might. Human beings *just like* friendship, and in all sorts of inarticulate ways friendship does them good. In the same way, humans also just like being physically touched, and being physically touched does them good. It is simply part of human nature to enjoy having other humans around. Provided they are not malevolent, and provided there is also some room to be alone sometimes, we just like having companions; we just like sharing our world with other human beings. We may call this phenomenon *animal compresence*.

Animal compresence doesn't seem to be a fact about humans that has any further explanation. Being touched releases hormones, endorphins for example, that have positive physiological effects. But this is not an explanation of why we like being touched or why being touched does us good.

It is, at most, an explanation of *how* being touched does us physical good. Again, the human enjoyment of being touched is plainly closely akin, evolutionarily speaking, to the enjoyment of touch that we see in the mutual grooming rituals displayed by chimpanzees, or by cats and dogs, or maybe even by oxpecker birds and rhinos. But, apart from the benefit of getting rid of parasites, which is not always what is achieved by grooming, this point just broadens the question out from 'Why do humans like being touched?' to 'Why do humans and all these other species too like being touched?' At some point it is reasonable to say: 'They just do.'

That being touched is good for humans, and pleasant for humans, is just a brute fact about them; it is a fact that explains other facts, not a fact that is itself explained by some 'deeper' fact. There are creatures that dislike physical contact (as such), but human beings are not such creatures. Broadly speaking, and aside from pleasure/pain, it is a basic fact about humans that they benefit from physical contact. Likewise with social contact of the very simple and basic kind that I am calling animal compresence. Humans just like having other humans around (and other species too – see next paragraph), in something like the same rather basic and unanalysable way that they like warmth, entertainment, pleasant scenery, hot baths, and the smell of fresh-ground coffee. *Why* do they like it? Well, they just do.

We should recognise animal compresence as the basis of the very real sense in which human–animal friendships are most certainly possible. Philosophers tend to struggle to explain how rational creatures like us can possibly be friends with a mere dog or cat. Everyone who isn't a philosopher, and even some people who are philosophers, know perfectly well that we *can* be friends with dogs or cats, and other kinds of animal too. And the notion of animal compresence gives us a first clue to how it is possible, and what it is like, to be friends with an animal. For a more spelled-out picture of what human–animal friendships are like, there is a rich literature of testimony to draw on: Rai Gaita's *The Philosopher's Dog* (2003), Mark Rowlands' *The Philosopher and the Wolf* (2008), and Gavin Maxwell's *Ring of Bright Water* (1960) are three obvious starting points.

The phenomenon of animal compresence shows how, at the simple animal level and at the level of the basic natural history of the species, we just are, as Aristotle said, social animals. But as I say, this doesn't stop us offering further explanations of what friendship and companionship give us, and how they benefit us. And here, too, we can tie these explanations to the natural history of human life. More about this in Chapter 7.

7   Being with Others

Being with others is an essential part of being human. Perhaps it begins as animal compresence and only later becomes other things such as the mutual awareness of minds; however, if so, the development of those other things is very quick and very early. Perhaps they too are actually there all along.

As I've argued at more length elsewhere (Chappell 2022b, Chapter 7): from the very beginning, our subjective experience as individual humans involves other individual humans, and involves them pervasively and constitutively. (As we've just seen, our experience often involves other animals too; in this Chapter I won't focus any further on human–animal friendships, but the possibility of such friend- ships continues to be a useful corrective to a lot of things that philosophers have said about being with others.) To be the kind of creatures that we are is to be shaped, both physically and mentally, by other people. After all, apart from anything else, 'other people' includes my biological parents, and/or those who parent me. We do not start off, each of us, in isolation, and only later discover other persons. Each of us becomes a self in a context set and shaped by others – quite literally 'set and shaped', in the case of those others who are *mothers*. So for us humans company precedes isolation; the *we* precedes the *I*.

Typically in contemporary moral psychology, exactly the opposite assumption is made. Sometimes, perhaps, it is made on utilitarian grounds, or as a result of the same individualistic mindset that also breeds utilitarianism (cp. Chapter 2). Typically philosophers assume that the *I* comes first, and the *we* of sociality is a kind of theoretical afterthought. It is assumed that we can formulate a coherent vision of what it is to be an agent that, from the start and by definition, abstracts away from such particularities as character, social position, relationships, sociology, and history. This is very obviously so in, for instance, John Rawls' theory of justice, where 'the self is prior to the ends which are affirmed by it' (1971, 560): for Rawls, 'we are free and independent selves, unbound by antecedent moral ties, capable of choosing our ends for ourselves' (Sandel 1994, 1768–1769). And these free and independent selves then come together as *reasonable bargainers* with each other: persons are reasonable when 'they are ready to propose principles and standards as fair terms of cooperation and to abide by them willingly, given the assurance that others will likewise do so' (Rawls 1993, 49).

But real persons, unlike Rawlsian ones, do not always appear in the world as in any degree 'free and independent', and never appear as *completely* 'free and independent' – still less as 'unbound by antecedent moral ties' or capable of reasonable bargaining by means of their own autonomous capacities from the word go. On the contrary, in real life all of us at all times are bound by antecedent moral ties, to the parents and families and communities and societies from which we (quite literally) come. And all of us at some times are neither free, nor independent, nor capable of choosing our ends – shared or individual, political or personal – for ourselves. This is so for everyone at the beginning of their lives. For most people who do not die suddenly, it is so at the end of their lives too. For anyone who is seriously ill for any length of time, it is so during that period of sickness, whenever it comes in their lives. And for some people, it is so throughout their lives.

Compare here the opening lines, and indeed the title, of Alasdair MacIntyre's *Dependent Rational Animals: Why Human Beings Need the Virtues*:

> We human beings are vulnerable to many kinds of affliction and most of us are at some time afflicted by serious ills. How we cope is only in small part up to us. It is most often to others that we owe our survival, let alone our flourishing, as we encounter bodily illness and injury, inadequate nutrition, mental defect and disturbance, and human aggression and neglect. This dependence on particular others for protection and sustenance is most obvious in early childhood and in old age. But between these first and last stages our lives are characteristically marked by longer or shorter periods of injury, illness, or other disablement and some among us are disabled for their entire lives.
>
> These two related sets of facts, those concerning our vulnerabilities ... and those concerning ... our dependence ... are so evidently of singular importance that it might seem that no account of the human condition whose authors hoped to achieve credibility could avoid giving them a central place. Yet the history of Western moral philosophy suggests otherwise. From Plato to Moore and since, [on the rare occasions] when the ill, the injured, and the otherwise disabled *are* presented in the pages of moral philosophy books, it is

almost always exclusively as possible subjects of
benevolence by moral agents who are themselves
presented as though they were continuously rational,
healthy, and untroubled. So we are invited, when we do
think of disability, to think of the disabled as 'them', as
other than 'us', as a separate class, not as ourselves as we
have been, sometimes are now, and may well be in
the future. (1999, 1–2)

Human vulnerability and dependence, MacIntyre
points out, are not incidental or accidental or unusual fea-
tures of human life. At both ends of life, and in between too,
they are entirely characteristic. About one end of life (the
end end), the climber Paul Pritchard put it well, after he had
suffered a serious head injury that left him with permanent
brain damage: 'In the end, we're all disabled.' As for the
other end (the beginning end), cases where humans are
vulnerable and dependent are not an afterthought that can
be put off 'at the initial stage'. They *are* the initial stage, and
quite literally so. Leaving these facts out of our account is
not a way of eliminating distractions from the 'fundamental
case' of human interaction. It is a fundamental misrepresen-
tation of the fundamental case, and of what it is actually like
for human beings to live, and so, of what it is like for them to
live together in a political community.

A realistic account of the human individual cannot
begin with Rational Man. It must begin somewhere else,
somewhere that does proper justice to the dependency of
each human individual on his or her familial, social, political, and communal background, and so, in the process,
captures the fundamental place in each human individual's

experience of *other* human individuals, and of each individual's vulnerability to these others.

A realistic account of the human individual, and of the place of other human individuals in any human individual's experience, should begin where the human individual begins. It should begin with the baby: 'The human infant is born social in the sense that his development will depend from the beginning upon patterns of interaction with elders. *He does not enter into that interaction as an individual partner ... infants only become individual partners gradually, as a result of those interactions*' (Kaye 1982, 29; italics added). Kaye's point is that 'parents create persons', not only in the reproductive sense that they 'make babies together', but also in the sense that a baby becomes an 'individual partner', a player in social interactions, *because her parents treat her as such*. She learns her self-awareness from them; she learns to look on herself *as* an individual partner in her interactions with her parents, because she picks up that that is how they look on her.

There is then a huge amount to say about how parents socialise their children – and more than one enormous academic literature dealing with precisely this. But let us focus on just one aspect of this vast topic, since it connects up with something I was discussing before: the notion of a role. The connection runs via the notion of a script, for elucidation of which we may look to the anthropologist Mary Douglas:

> As a social animal, man is a ritual animal ... Without the letters of condolence, telegrams of congratulations and

> even occasional postcards, the friendship of a separated friend is not a social reality. It has no existence without the rites of friendship. Social rituals create a reality which would be nothing without them. It is not too much to say that ritual is more to society than words are to thoughts. For it is very possible to know something and then find words for it. But it is impossible to have social relations without symbolic acts. (1966, 77–78)

Douglas's 'ritual' or 'symbolic act' is my 'script' (a term already used in this sense by Kwame Anthony Appiah in 1994). A script is a motif, a pattern, a routine, a theme, a meme, a programme, a way of acting or being or feeling, a role. Scripts appear in the stories that we tell or hear; they appear there because, more fundamentally, they also appear in the lives that those stories reflect. Scripts appear in, and they shape and frame and direct, both our personal deliberations and our actions; so they're psychological realities. And they appear in, and they shape and frame and direct, both our collective deliberations and our interactions; so they're sociological realities.

Here is a small-scale example of a script: there is in our society – and therefore in the minds and manners of all normally socialised members of our society – a script about how to behave when introduced to someone. You smile, you make eye contact, you say 'Hello, pleased to meet you, I'm Sophie Grace' (at least, you do if that's your name), and you watch the other person's body language to see whether they want to shake hands with you. (In our society this is something of a grey area; some people will, some people won't, and context makes a difference too.)

Now scripts come in smaller- and in larger-scale varieties, and a script can be complex and large-scale enough to deserve to be called both a script and also a role. This is how it is with the case just considered, the case of introducing oneself to a stranger, which is one of the few ways in which our society ritualises the opening of a relationship; as noted above, other societies go much further in this kind of direction with their highly elaborate codes of hospitality. It is also how it is with fatherhood and friendship, which are likewise both roles and (generative of) scripts. We have a complicated nexus of expectations about what it is to be a friend or a father. Some of these expectations extend over the whole of a person's life, and some of them are relatively small-scale. A father is supposed always to 'be there' for his children, from the moment they're born (and indeed before) to the moment he dies (and indeed after). In that respect, the script of fatherhood is as large-scale as scripts get. But it has small-scale components too which are themselves also scripts, like reading school reports, giving out pocket money and impulsive fivers, exchanging Christmas presents, cuddling, providing a free taxi service, and telling stories.

Likewise with friendship. Being someone's friend means (more strictly: means *in our society*) wanting to have animal compresence with her, being interested in her, wanting to hang out with her, being willing to help her when she needs it, and so on, for the long term: in cases of *deep* friendship, for the whole of our lives. But there are small scripts that friends follow too, and follow *qua* friends: buying each other drinks, hugging when they meet instead of shaking hands, keeping up the banter-flow on social media, remembering each other's birthdays, writing thank-you letters, and the rest. And so, from the beginning of our lives as beings who are socialised by others, we gradually become beings who socialise ourselves – and eventually others too.

There is, of course, far more than this to say about the natural history of friendship – and the cultural history and social anthropology that it leads us to. But there are two main points that this swift and no doubt rough sketch of such a natural history serves to demonstrate, and I want to close this chapter by stating them explicitly.

The first point is that friendship has a broad sense, simply as the benevolent companionship of others over time, and a variety of narrower senses – different socially articulated ways of expressing and living out that benevolence and that companionship, which come to life in the scripts and indeed the roles that any given society clothes them in.

The second point is that we should avoid generalising from these 'narrow' particular social articulations of friendship to the broad notion of friendship itself; we should also avoid generalising from any of those 'narrow' articulations of friendship that are natural to economically well-off, middle-aged intellectuals such as we philosophers tend to be, to other 'narrow' articulations of friendship that we academics find less natural. C. S. Lewis said that 'Friendship is an affair of disentangled minds' (1960, 67), and no doubt Lewis's friendships were. But few people are that cerebral. Remember here the point about 'observer interference' that I noted in Chapter 3: that with a topic like friendship, there is no clear divide between observation and recommendation, description and prescription. When a philosopher says what she thinks friendship *is*, she is always also saying what she thinks friendship *should be*.

No doubt friendship in the broad sense is itself a role, albeit of a vague sort, and can be the source of many more particular and more definite specifications of *kinds* of friendship as narrower and more clearly defined *kinds* of role. But we should not allow ourselves either to confuse the narrow notion of friendship with the broad, nor to impose on others whatever kinds of narrower notion we ourselves may find congenial. For others may have other ways than ours of articulating a narrow and specific notion of friendship; their notions may suit them just fine, even though they would not suit us. Nor, again, should we allow ourselves to become trapped by any of those narrower versions, in the way that (as I said in Chapter 1) 'blokeyness' can become a trap for men in our society.

This second point might help us to see what is wrong with what are perhaps the two most famous taxonomies in the history of the philosophy of friendship: C. S. Lewis's, and Aristotle's. Lewis's taxonomy divides love into four, and sees friendship as one of the four varieties of love. (The other three varieties are romantic love; family love; and *agape*, spiritual or Christian love.) Aristotle's taxonomy divides friendship into three, depending on what motivates the friendship ('advantage', or 'honour', or 'virtue').

Formally speaking, these two taxonomies are consistent – they could both be true at the same time. But while there is certainly something to be said for both of them, I want to suggest that the two taxonomies share an important failing: they both take as universal what is, in fact, decidedly local. And besides this shared failing, both have other weaknesses too – weaknesses that are important and illuminating, and have much to tell us about the nature both of friendship, and of love.

In the next two chapters, I offer a brief critique of each of them in turn.

8   Lewis's Four Loves – and Nygren's Two

P erhaps the most influential and familiar taxonomy of the varieties of love – a quick bit of googling shows its striking prevalence even today, nearly sixty-five years after publication – comes from C. S. Lewis's 1960 classic of popular theology, *The Four Loves*.

This book is surely far oftener referenced than actually read. Indeed this superficial acquaintance may be part of what keeps it popular, given what even a Lewis fan like myself can only see as problematic when we take a closer look. In particular there is the embarrassing (one might be kind and say 'dated') misogyny and homophobia of significant parts of the book, especially in Lewis's chapters on friendship and eros. The very idea of homosexual friendships is crudely and rudely dismissed on pp.57–60. The theses that women are engaged in a 'war on friendship' and that, at least in Lewis's sense of 'friendship', most women of his time are not even capable of it, are quite seriously propounded on pp.68–72. (Lewis 1960, 68: 'Where men are educated and women not, where one sex works and the other is idle [!!!], or where they do totally different work, they will usually have nothing to be friends about.') And then on pp.97–98 we find that St Paul's notorious doctrine of the 'headship of the man' (1 Corinthians 11.3, Ephesians 5.23) has for Lewis the consequence that husbands as such are to wives as kings are to

85

beggar-girls. And this is not to mention Lewis's relentless pontificating about all manner of unrelated issues that his own words plainly show he doesn't understand at all: politics and science, for instance.

Our culture today has an unfortunate tendency to cancel the baby along with the bathwater. Despite its alarming flaws, *The Four Loves* is undeniably a marvellously perceptive book about many things. Lewis's gifts as a moral phenomenologist, a chronicler of human ethical experience, are undeniable, and his basic idea is interesting.

The 'four loves' are *storge* (family/familiar affection), *philia* (friendship), *eros* (sexual/romantic love), and *agape* (unconditional, sacrificial, self-giving love, specifically Christian love). A separate distinction that Lewis also makes, and which intersects with this fourfold taxonomy, is his distinction between need-love and gift-love. In making this latter distinction, Lewis was influenced by another famous twentieth-century moderate-Protestant writer on love as *agape* and *eros*: the Danish theologian Anders Nygren. ('He has shaken me up extremely': C. S. Lewis, Letter to Janet Spens, 8 January 1935; See Hinds 2016.) In Nygren's 1930 classic book on the subject he famously makes a somewhat neo-Kantian distinction between *agape* and *eros* – self-sacrificial love and demanding love. Lewis tells us in the introduction to *The Four Loves* that his original plan in writing *The Four Loves*, thirty years after Nygren, was to model it on this distinction, and to praise gift-love while disparaging need-love. But Lewis found the subject matter resistant to this simple division – he couldn't make it fit into those two categories. So, very sensibly, he reframed his approach around four categories instead.

Certainly any level-headed reader is likely to find Nygren's twofold taxonomy of need-love and gift-love inadequate as a full account of friendship. But the fourfold taxonomy that Lewis eventually preferred to Nygren's is problematic too.

For one thing, both taxonomies are historically dubious. Despite the claim-staking implicit in their use of Greek terminology, neither Nygren's nor Lewis's taxonomy has any obvious historical basis in ancient Greek thought, either pagan or Christian. Neither Plato nor Aristotle registers anything like Nygren's or Lewis's distinctions. Plato's *Republic* distinguishes three kinds of desire, according to whether they derive from *epithumia* or *thumos* or *logos* (brute desire, honourable passion, and reason). Plato's *Symposium* (180b, 209c) distinguishes two kinds of eros. One is a 'heavenly' *eros*: homosexual, tending to transcend individual or physical passion, metaphorically procreative of beautiful ideas, and oriented directly to *to kalon*, The Beautiful, or *to Agathon*, The Good. The other is a 'popular' *eros*: heterosexual, individual, physical, literally procreative of actual children, and oriented at best to a good refracted through bodily and worldly life. And Aristotle's *Nicomachean Ethics* – as we'll see in Chapter 9 – distinguishes three kinds of friendship, based respectively on advantage, on honour, and on virtue. Plato and Aristotle come no closer than this to presenting any taxonomy of the varieties of love at all, let alone ones like Lewis's or Nygren's.

Lewis's and Nygren's distinctions are not in the Bible either. And here, if the reader will forgive me a spot of philological analysis, it is worthwhile to look closely at the actual Greek words that the New Testament uses.

87

Certainly the commonest word in the Greek New Testament for 'love' is *agape*. In the Summary of the Law (Matthew 22.37–39), we read: 'You shall love the Lord your God with all your heart, and all your soul, and all your understanding, and your neighbour as yourself.' Here 'you shall love' is the cognate verb, *agapeseis*. Moreover, the word *agape* and its cognates are especially common in the books written by the disciple John (or his followers), and these are certainly the most ethereally spiritual and otherworldly parts of the New Testament. So it is certainly possible that, as Lewis and Nygren think, the New Testament writers' tendency to prefer the word *agape* to the more ordinary and usual word *philia* reflects a wish to imply that there is something distinctive, and superior, about Christian love. Perhaps it also marks an association of ideas with the early Christians' Eucharistic 'love meals' – evening parties which they called *agape*s (see one reading of 2 Peter 2.13) – although it is pretty clear, as we see from 1 Corinthians 11, that these sometimes got rowdy and even licentious.

All the same, the plain truth is that the New Testament observes no hard and fast distinction of any kind between *agape* and *philia*, not even in the parts of it written by John (or 'school of John'). Often, in fact, these nouns (and cognates such as the nouns *philos* and *agapêtos*, and the verbs *agapan* and *philein*) seem straightforwardly interchangeable. When Jesus says at John 15.15 that the disciples are not his servants but his friends, his word is *philoi*. At 1 Peter 4.12, the writer's audience of Christian believers are addressed as *agapêtoi*; translators of this word into English are about evenly divided between 'beloved' and 'dear friends'. Again, in John 20.2 the disciple 'whom Jesus loved' is *hon ephilei ho Iêsous*, but in John 13.23 he is *hon êgapa ho Iêsous*. Or even more strikingly: in John 21.15, Jesus's question to Peter is *agapais me*? ('Do you love me?') and Peter's reply – in the very same verse – is *su oidas hoti philô se* ('You know that I love you'). It is quite implausible to see these passages as distinguishing *philein* and *agapan* in any principled or systematic way. On the contrary, they pretty clearly treat the verbs as synonyms.

I turn to Lewis's other two loves, *storgê* and *erôs*. *Storge* is certainly not, *pace* Lewis (1960, 33), what 'the Greeks called' family affection; the normal term for that is simply *philia*. The word *storge* is not very common in classical Greek, and it is not in the New Testament at all. At Romans 12.10, there is one occurrence of a compound *philostorgoi*, 'affectionately loving'; at Romans 1.31 and 2 Timothy 3.3 we get the compound *astorgoi*, 'lacking in natural affection'; however, that is as close as the Bible gets to even using the word. And in any case, the standard lexicon of classical Greek, Liddell-Scott-Jones (LSJ), tells us that *storgê* can sometimes mean sexual love (as indeed can *agapê*).

Meanwhile, the word *erôs* does not occur at all in the New Testament. Not only that, *erôs* is replaced by other terms even in places where we might expect it. When St Paul tells husbands to love their wives in Ephesians 5.28, his verb is not *eran* but *agapan*. If we apply a distinction like Nygren's or Lewis's to this, we will presumably conclude that Paul is telling Corinthian husbands not to feel sexually toward their wives, but to relate to them in a spirit of righteous high-minded sacrifice. Such an instruction might make sense given the possibility of a sufficiently puritanical mindset, and/or a sufficiently tiresome spouse. Still, if only for the sake of the marriages in question, one rather hopes that that possibility was not actual.

So the historical pedigree in the Bible and classical thought that Lewis and Nygren claimed for their distinctions is really very questionable indeed. Still, mightn't those distinctions be attractive anyway, independently of their historical pedigree? Clearly Nygren is right that, simply as a matter of common human experience, there is a range, within love, from merely physiological need or appetite to something 'higher', 'purer', more generously giving, more sacrificial. And no doubt Lewis is right to see friendship, romance, familiar affection, and sheerly altruistic love as kinds of love that are often, in practice, broadly distinguishable – though as I keep saying, they can and do also overlap a lot, and the social realisations of all four varieties can be and have been extremely various. But one serious question for Lewis and his fans is whether his particular taxonomy of love has any particular advantage over other possible taxonomies. Why couldn't we use his taxonomy in one social and cultural context, and some other taxonomy in another?

Another, and connected, question is how deep the distinctions really are between Lewis's four kinds. Obviously, as Lewis himself observes, someone's love for someone else might involve more than one of his four loves; it might even involve all four of them at once. But then it is also obviously possible that some or all of those four loves might be so blended together within a given relationship that it is really quite hard, and decidedly artificial, to separate them out again. And it gets hard to ignore the question why *this* taxonomy, the taxonomy of the 'four loves', is the one that we should emphasise above all other possible taxonomies. When my friendship with John starts to be a romance as well as a friendship, that is certainly a basic change in our relationship. But there are plenty of other basic changes that might happen. For instance, John and I might start playing golf as well as only seeing each other at the politics discussion group, or John and I might become friends in the real world as well as online. Why not say that *these* are changes in our relationship that deserve to be reflected in our taxonomy of the kinds of love?

Almost the next book that Lewis wrote after *The Four Loves* was his most enduringly valuable and most moving book of all, *A Grief Observed* (1961). In it he remembers his own four-year marriage to Helen Joy Davidman in words like these:

> For those four years H and I feasted on love; every mode
> of it – solemn and merry, romantic and realistic,
> sometimes as dramatic as a thunderstorm, sometimes as
> comfortable and unemphatic as putting on your slippers.
> No cranny of heart or body remained unsatisfied ... [In
> some high spiritual sense perhaps we were] two circles
> that touched. But those two circles, above all the points at
> which they touched, are the very thing I am mourning
> for, homesick for, famished for. You tell me 'She goes on.'
> But my heart and body are crying out, come back, come
> back. Be a circle touching my circle on the plane of
> Nature ... the thing I want is exactly the thing I can

never get. The old life, the jokes, the drinks, the
arguments, the love-making, the tiny, heart-
breaking commonplace. (Lewis 1961, 10, 22)

From this beautiful description of his marriage to Joy, it
seems clear that in Lewis's own life and experience his 'four
loves' were thoroughly blended: their marriage was to them
eros, and friendship, and *storge*, and *agape* all together and
all at once. (And plainly their marriage blended need-love
and gift-love, too.) This does not make it impossible to
distinguish the four loves, but it does undermine the idea
that distinguishing them is all we need to do to understand
love – or friendship.

A further question about Lewis's taxonomy is more
searching still. It is whether, in fact, what he calls *agape* is
really love at all. (Ironically, Lewis himself has a roughly
converse worry – that only 'gift-love' is truly love, and 'need-
love' is just need.) His kind of 'sheerly altruistic love' sounds
so superior, *so* spiritual, *so* universal, *so* impartial and impersonal, and *so* unaffected by the particularities of its object,
the person whom it is love of, that we might actually suspect
that *agape* is not so much love as *benevolence*. I shall argue
further in Chapter 10 that benevolence is not love, *precisely
because* it is impersonal and impartial.

As, in fact, we see from Lewis's own impassioned
description of his marriage, love (real love) is inevitably
modified and toned by the nature of its object. My love for
John is necessarily love *for him*: it gets its character from his
character – and from mine. But my benevolence towards
John is not necessarily either *my* benevolence, nor *towards*

John. Benevolence is not *constituted* by whose benevolence it is, and towards whom. At most, these factors make benevolence well targeted or otherwise. Benevolence towards John is simply about wanting and aiming, in a general and impersonal way, to bring good things to John, as I might (and presumably should) want to bring good things to anyone. By contrast, my loving John is essentially *my* loving, and essentially loving *of John*.

Now this difference between benevolence and love might well seem to tell, not in favour of heavenly benevolence, but in favour of down-to-earth love. Consider Sir Galahad, in T. H. White's marvellous Arthurian novel *The Once and Future King*. Here is Galahad, described in a conversation between the ploddingly kind but essentially unheroic King Arthur, and the wildly heroic but secretly sinful Sir Lancelot:

> 'I know hardly anything about Galahad,' [said Arthur,] 'except that everybody dislikes him.'
> 'Dislikes him?'
> 'They complain about his being inhuman.'
> Lancelot considered his cup.
> 'He is inhuman,' he said at last. 'But why should he be human? Are angels supposed to be human? . . . Do you think that if the Archangel Michael were to come here this minute, he would say 'What charming weather we are having today!'? . . . People talk far too much. Where I have been, and where Galahad is, it is a waste of time to have 'manners'. Manners are only needed between people, to keep their empty affairs in order . . . So you can understand how Galahad may have seemed inhuman, and mannerless, and so on, to the people who were

> buzzing and clacking about him. He was far away in his
> spirit, living on desert islands, in silence, with eternity.'
> (White 1958, 498)

Thus the 'human' Lancelot praises the 'inhuman' Galahad –
who is also, of course, Lancelot's own son, and the direct
result of Lancelot's own original sin, the fumbling sexual
encounter with Elaine whereby Lancelot, as he sees it, so lost
his purity that he might as well go on and become an
adulterer with Guinevere as well. Such virtue and goodness
as Galahad's may well if you like be heavenly and supernat-
ural. As Lancelot and Arthur bring out, that does not make
Galahad any more humanly understandable – or likeable; it
does not make Galahad's holiness into *love*. It is not for
nothing that Lancelot is one of the three main protagonists
in *The Once and Future King*, whereas Galahad is only a
minor character – and one who, shortly after the episode
that Lancelot is here relating, becomes so holy that he
evanesces entirely.

Both for C. S. Lewis and for T. H. White, the
contrast between heavenly *agape* and more natural human
loves can seem like a contrast between love as we know it
and something so remote and superhuman that, while
undoubtedly good, it is not sufficiently *human* to count as
love at all. We might be reminded of William Blake's marvellous remark in *Jerusalem*: 'Whoever would do good must
do it in minute particulars; general good is the plea of the
scoundrel, the hypocrite, and the flatterer' (1804, f. 55, ll.
48–53, 60–66). The disfavour with which we might view
such a general and universal notion of 'holy, heavenly love'

as *agape* sometimes seems to be, might also remind us of the Latin equivalent of Lewis's Greek term *agape*: namely *charity*, a word that, as Charles Dickens, George Bernard Shaw, and George Orwell often point out, has come to have some very dark associations.

Lewis exalts *agape* as a distinctly Christian sort of love, and therefore the best of all. Long before Lewis St Gregory of Nazianzus famously remarked about the Christian doctrine of the incarnation: 'For that which He has not assumed He has not healed; but that which is united to His Godhead is also saved' (The Advent Project n. d.). If God is to love humans, as Christianity says he does, then that must mean not merely God's wishing them well in a general way, but God's actually loving *them*: each of them distinctly, as the particular and unique humans that they are. The banquet of heaven should not be a kind of celestial soup-kitchen, benevolently doling out the same nourishing (but perhaps monotonous) fare of beneficence to all alike. Rather, the menu for the Wedding Feast of the Lamb should be not only *à la carte*, but bespoke and individualised to each and every diner.

One corollary of this theological point about love and friendship is very striking. It is that if friendship with God is possible, as Christianity has always claimed, then not even friendship with God will be *agape* in the sense just defined. If some of the most familiar and central Christian teachings are true then the believer's relationship with God (or Jesus, or however we want to put it) will be actually a *relationship*, and one characterised by second-personal interaction and not merely by being on the receiving end of massive cosmic benevolence. It will not be a case of *agape* but of friendship – or possibly even something like the love found in a marriage. It will be, as my rough definition of friendship has it, 'benevolent companionship over time', where companionship means *mutual second-personality*: it means that I see someone else as a person who sees me as a person. (For Christians to say that friendship is possible with God is, then, exactly this. Their claim is that it is possible for me to see God as a person who sees me as a person.)

This may, perhaps, sound rather soppily fluffy-evangelical. Yet there are some very hard-headed and intellectually rigorous non-evangelical Christians who are happy to say something very like it:

> To be a Christian is to know, however deep down, and however much we forget from day to day, that our relationship with Christ is everything. Perhaps too many Christians bang on too loudly about their 'personal relationship with Jesus', so that it sounds fake and superficial. But equally, perhaps, too many Christians keep quiet about it. Because it is true that this is the heart of it – everything else is no more than commentary. And to work on that relationship – to give it 'quality time', to pay attention, to listen, to try to please the Beloved – is no less important than in a human marriage. (John 2001, 54)

> I asked one of the monks how he could sum up, in a few words, his way of life. He paused a moment and asked 'Have you ever been in love?' I said, 'Yes.' A large Fernandel smile spread across his face. 'Eh bien,' he said, 'c'est exactement pareil . . .' (Fermor 1957, 39)

After all, Jesus himself – though he seems to have rejected at least some kinds of family tie, and though he may have proclaimed a love that did not discriminate between men or women, Jews or Gentiles, sinners or holy men, children or adults – nonetheless had *friends*. He shared a communal and mendicant life with a group of particular companions and followers, his disciples – whose numbers are seventy if you count the larger looser group, and twelve if you count only the apostles. And even among the Twelve who were his close friends, Jesus clearly favoured some of them over others. Only three disciples went up with him on the mount of transfiguration; only one disciple was the one 'whom Jesus loved'.

Whether or not we go with these objections to Lewis's notion of *agape* (I do), and whether or not we are prepared to entertain the possibility of friendship with God (I am), at any rate we can say that Lewis's taxonomy of the four loves is not philosophically or ethically compulsory. With or without the backing of the New Testament and classical Greek thought, we don't *have* to see the varieties of love as he distinguishes them, nor do we have to adhere to his distinctions in our own lives.

For to tell the truth, Lewis tends to treat friendship not just as typically a male affair, but moreover as one that typically occurs between well-read middle-class intellectuals like himself and the others in the famous 1930s–1950s Oxford coterie the Inklings. Of such a friendship group, he writes, any one of the members might feel proud and humbled to be part of it:

> Especially when the whole group is together, each
> bringing out all that is best, or wisest, or funniest, in all

the others. Those are the golden sessions; when four or five of us after a hard day's walking have come to our inn; when our slippers are on, our feet spread out towards the blaze, and our drinks at our elbows; when the whole world, and something beyond the world, opens itself to our minds as we talk; and no one has any claim or any responsibility for another, but all are freemen and equals as if we had met half an hour ago, while at the same time an affection mellowed by the years enfolds us. Life – natural life – has no better gift to give. Who could have deserved it? (Lewis 1960, 68)

This is a beautiful little vignette of what it must have been like to be one of the Inklings. (By no accident, it also sounds a bit like what it would be like to be a hobbit; in times of peace, I mean.) Absolutely this is one possible inflection of the good of friendship, one possible version of what friendship can be for us. But only one, and one that is highly particular in time and place and atmosphere and preoccupations. Nothing wrong with that, of course; as Lewis himself observes in Aphorism 15, there is nothing more individual, and individualistic, than the particular friendship. But just for that reason there is all too often a danger of projecting outwards from our own case towards over-ambitious universal claims about every case. Here and elsewhere, Lewis does seem to fall into this danger.

In that respect, Lewis's account of the four loves shares a defect with Aristotle's account of the three kinds of friendship, to which I turn next.

9 Aristotle's Three Kinds of *Philia* – and Aristotle's Will

In the *Nicomachean Ethics* Books VIII–IX, Aristotle is the author of an immensely influential study of *philia* – friendship, as it is usually translated, though I have already suggested that this is a misleading translation, and shall be saying more about the point in a moment. Aristotle famously divides *philia* into three kinds. The first and 'highest' of these three kinds is the focal and paradigmatic case of *philia*; the other two kinds are 'lower' and derivative cases, which may sometimes perhaps only count as *philia* in an extended or metaphorical sense (*kat' analogian*, in Aristotle's terminology). The focal case is 'the friendship of virtue', a relationship of intimate companionship and shared moral/intellectual endeavour between educated and aristocratic men. The two derivative cases of *philia* that most interest Aristotle are 'the friendship of honour', typified by partnerships formed between free adult men in order to achieve the ends of honour such as political office or military or sporting success, and 'the friendship of advantage', of which friendships based on amusement or pleasure, and on money-making, would both apparently count for Aristotle as examples.

Now this is all decidedly suspect. One reason why has to do with Aristotle's rather artificial-seeming threefold division of the types of friendship. We know from Book 1 of the *Nicomachean Ethics* that Aristotle is strongly inclined to classify the main kinds of thing that typically motivate human beings into three closely parallel categories: (1) money or pleasure, (2) honour, and (3) virtue or the good. This classification of motivations is clearly what underlies Aristotle's corresponding classification of types of friendship in Book 8. But both classifications are artificial and schematic, as a moment's reflection on category (1) will show. 'Money or pleasure' is hardly a *single* objective for us to pursue, so why does Aristotle class it as *one* kind of motivation?

That is of course a rhetorical question, but actually it has a very obvious answer. This answer lies in Plato's *Republic*, Book 4, where (as we've seen) Plato famously divides the human *psyche* and its motivations into three – Reason, Passion, and Desire (*logos, thumos, epithumia*) – and uses this threefold division of the *psyche* for his own highly schematic purposes in constructing an analogy between how things are in human psychology, and how things should therefore (?) be in human society. Aristotle has a very different account of the *psyche* from Plato; nonetheless, he simply takes over Plato's schematic division of types of motivation. We should treat his use of this schematism with the same suspicion that we rightly attach to Plato's use of it – the same suspicion that is always applicable when philosophers borrow their accounts of reality from each other, since when they do that there is always the risk of their not bothering to look back at reality itself to check for verisimilitude. Aristotle's threefold division of the types of *philia* does not even seem particularly convincing as an account of what friendships between adult men looked like in his own society. There is all the less reason to think that his threefold division can be illuminatingly applied to our very different society.

The fact that all three of Aristotle's categories of *philia* are kinds of friendship or association between free adult men brings us to the second main reason why his account of friendship is suspect. The point here is one that we have seen before, but keep needing to come back to: it is that the ancient Greek word *philia* normally has a much broader sense than the English word 'friendship'. Unlike our word 'friendship' as it is usually understood, *philia* can mean any kind of affectionate relationship between people, including familial and erotic relationships. What is noteworthy about Aristotle's treatment of *philia* in the *Nicomachean Ethics* is that Aristotle is not really interested in that breadth of meaning. In 8.7–12 he does discuss *philia* between 'unequals' such as parents and children, husbands and wives, and even owners and slaves. But the central case of friendship, and the one to which he makes all other cases relative, is high-minded intellectual friendship between adult, free, and preferably aristocratic men.

Here it is interesting to contrast Aristotle's philosophical account of *philia* in the *Nicomachean Ethics* with some of the known facts about Aristotle's biography. (We are unusually lucky with Aristotle, in that we do actually know a bit about his life; this isn't at all the case with most ancient Greek authors.) We certainly know that friendships with other intellectual and idealistic men were an important part of Aristotle's life-story. Both his parents died when he was about thirteen, so that he was brought up for four years or so by his brother-in-law (his older sister's husband), one Proxenus, and after that by Plato himself, in his Academy. Aristotle tells us in *Nicomachean Ethics* 1.6 that his relationship with Plato was a strong and deep friendship, and it seems to have been one of the main formative events of his life. It may or may not have been a homosexual romantic attachment of the kind then usual – whether physical or 'platonic' – with the older Plato as *erastes* (the lover, the active role) and the younger Aristotle as *erwmenos* (the beloved, the passive). When Aristotle was older he himself, if we are to believe the decidedly unreliable Suda, took the role of *erastes* to an *erwmenos* of his own, one Palaephatus, like himself a scholar and writer.

But important as these male and intellectual relationships naturally were to him, we know perfectly well, even at this distance of time, that in his own life Aristotle certainly did not experience *philia* only with other clever and idealistic literary men. The key evidence here is Aristotle's will (322 BC), which has come down to us in full. It is a remarkable document. When our focus is on Aristotle's philosophy of friendship – or rather, his philosophy of the broader category of *philia* – his will rewards the closest attention.

Aristotle begins the will by making careful dispositions for his young daughter Pythias (whose mother, also called Pythias, had died about ten years before) and for his son Nicomachus (whose mother was Aristotle's slave/concubine Herpyllis, who survived him). Both his children are put under the guardianship of Aristotle's nephew Nicanor (his sister's son), whom he directs to marry Pythias when she comes of age. (This sounds like an overbearing instruction to us, but the point of it is to protect Pythias.) Of Herpyllis, Aristotle writes, with a note of warning in his tone, that

> The executors and Nicander should remember that Herpyllis has been good to me. If she wishes to marry, they should give her to someone worthy of me [again, the point is to ensure Herpyllis' position]; and they should take care also of her other needs. In addition to the other gifts that she has received previously they should give her a talent of silver, from the estate, and three female slaves, if she wishes, and the female slave that she has at present, and the slave Pyrrhaeus. If she wishes to live in Chalcis, she is to have the guest-cottage by the garden. If she wishes to live at Stagira, she is to have my father's house. Whichever of the two she chooses, the executors are to equip it with furniture that seems to them suitable and that Herpyllis approves. (Aristotle, 332 BC)

Aristotle evidently foresees that Herpyllis, a mere slave-girl until he took her into his bed after the death of Pythias, stands to lose status sharply when he himself dies. So in his will he does everything that he can from the grave to protect her, and to ensure that she retains command of at least some of Aristotle's various houses. Above all, he is protecting her from a return to the state of slavery. And though it is part of his protection of Herpyllis to give her some slaves of her own, some of the other slaves that Aristotle had in his household do much better:

> Nicanor shall see that the slave Myrmex shall be returned to his family in a manner worthy of me with the property that we got from him. Ambracis also is to be freed, and

103

when my daughter marries, she shall be given
500 drachmas and the female slave she has at present . . .
When my daughter is married, Tachon shall be freed,
and also Philon, and Olympios, and his son. The
executors are not to sell any of the slaves who looked
after me, but to employ them. When they reach the
appropriate age, they should set them free as
they deserve. (Aristotle, 332 BC)

Aristotle seems to have been more inclusive in his
living than in his philosophising, for Aristotle was clearly
someone for whom affectionate relationships – relationships
of *philia* – even with slaves were not only possible but actual.
Yet in *Politics* Book 1, Aristotle makes some notorious
pronouncements on the irrationality and subhumanity of
slaves, and similar remarks are also there in *Nicomachean
Ethics* 8.11 (1161b3–5): 'A slave is a tool that happens to be
animate, just as a tool is a slave that happens to be inanimate; so there can be no *philia* for a slave as such, though
there can be for a slave as a human.'

Aristotle is well known for being the first philosopher to have a clear technical term to express the idea that
there might be very different ways of looking at any single
thing. The term is *êi* in ancient Greek, *qua* in the Latin
translations of Aristotle; the best English equivalent is probably 'considered as'. So, as Aristotle points out, we can look
at a statue *considered as* a statue, or *considered as* a lump of
bronze, or *considered as* an image of Pericles: *qua, qua, qua.*
Or we can inquire into the nature of existing things *considered as* they occur in zoology or politics, or into existing
things *considered in their own right*; this latter is what

Aristotle means by calling metaphysics 'the science of being *qua* being' (*Metaphysics*). We might say that in Aristotle's philosophy slaves are only considered *qua* tools. Yet here in Aristotle's will, it is just the other way round: at least some slaves are only considered *qua* human beings.

Nor was Aristotle – considered as a person – as universally and categorically disdainful of women as Aristotle – considered as a philosopher – often seems to have been. In the last paragraph of his will, Aristotle is very careful about the usual requirements of religious observance towards various members of his family, and gives a particular, and rather moving, place in his directions to the memory both of Nicanor's mother – Aristotle's sister – and of his own mother:

> The executors are to see that the images Gryllion has
> been commissioned to make are set up when they are
> finished: these are of Nicanor and of Proxenus, which
> I had meant to have commissioned, and of Nicanor's
> mother and the image of Arimnestos that has been
> completed, as a memorial to him, since he died childless.
> They should dedicate my mother's statue of Demeter at
> Nemea, or wherever they think best. (Aristotle, 332 BC)

Again, near the end of his will, Aristotle says something that is almost an allusion to Socrates' famous shrugging off, in Plato's *Phaedo*, of the question 'What shall we do with your body after your execution?' – but he absolutely doesn't share the coldness towards his womenfolk that Socrates displays in the *Phaedo*. Aristotle tells his executors that he doesn't care where he is buried, so long as he shares his grave with his first wife Pythias: 'Wherever they put my tomb, they should collect and place the bones of Pythias, as she herself requested' (Aristotle, 332 BC).

Overall, the evidence of his will is that Aristotle was perfectly capable of following one set of ideas in his philosophical works about friendship with women and slaves, while actually living in line with quite another set of ideas. (It shows something similar about Aristotle and religion, too. The will's last lines tell us that Aristotle, despite the lofty necessitarian theology and the bizarrely self-absorbed deity of his *Metaphysics*, was a man who made petitionary prayers to the gods for others' safe-keeping on journeys, and sealed his prayers with a votary's oaths: 'Because Nicanor returned safely, he should put up stone statues four cubits high in Stagira to Zeus the Preserver and Athena the Preserver, in fulfilment of my vow' Aristotle, 332 BC.) Aristotle's will makes it very clear that he had close relationships, indeed friendships, not only with his wife and children, but with his wider family and even with at least some of his slaves. And all of these relationships were, as I have pointed out, well covered by the normal sense of the ancient Greek word *philia*.

It is only Aristotle's philosophical theory of *philia* that moves us away from these human realities, into a realm where cases of *philia* that are not intellectual friendships between very clever free adult men are at best secondary and derivative cases, and most of the time not even worthy of notice. Perhaps the moral is that we should, at least sometimes, give a little less weight to Aristotle's rather narrow and exclusive moral theory of *philia* and a little more weight to the much wider and more inclusive place that *philia* had in Aristotle's own life and ethical experience.

10 Friendship, Love, and Second-Personality

Aristotle's and C. S. Lewis's systematising theories of friendship both face some of the same objections, and two in particular. First, they treat what is really only local to their own social and historical contexts as if it were universal and natural. Secondly and connectedly, their own prejudices are all too visible in what they choose to centre, and what they choose to marginalise or ignore.

What Aristotle and Lewis are surely right about, on the other hand, is that friendship is indeed a kind of love. So maybe, at this point, it is worthwhile to think a bit about love.

Once upon a time love was something of a taboo subject in analytical philosophy – almost as if analytical philosophers were uncomfortable with anything that gets too personal. So, for example, Iris Murdoch begins her 1962 essay 'The Idea of Perfection' with the simple and, at the time, accurate complaint that 'though contemporary philosophers constantly talk of freedom they rarely talk of love' (1970, 1). And it is central to her project in her 1970 book *The Sovereignty of Good*, of which 'The Idea of Perfection' is the first third, to answer her own complaint by presenting a form of ethics that is centred on the notion of love.

Also in 1962 Peter Strawson wrote this, in his celebrated essay 'Freedom and Resentment':

We should think of the many different kinds of relationship which we can have with other people – as sharers of a common interest; as members of the same family; as colleagues; as friends; as lovers; as chance parties to an enormous range of transactions and encounters. Then we should think, in each of these connections in turn, and in others, of the kind of importance we attach to the attitudes and intentions towards us of those who stand in these relationships to us, and of the kinds of reactive attitudes and feelings to which we ourselves are prone. In general, we demand some degree of goodwill or regard on the part of those who stand in these relationships to us, though the forms we require it to take vary widely in different connections. The range and intensity of our reactive attitudes towards goodwill, its absence or its opposite vary no less widely. I have mentioned, specifically, resentment and gratitude; and they are a usefully opposed pair. But, of course, there is a whole continuum of reactive attitude and feeling stretching on both sides of these and – the most comfortable area – in between them. The object of these commonplaces is to try to keep before our minds something it is easy to forget when we are engaged in philosophy, especially in our cool, contemporary style, viz. what it is actually like to be involved in ordinary interpersonal relationships, ranging from the most intimate to the most casual. (1962, section 3)

It is interesting that Strawson includes here a remark in passing that seems to register a preparedness to distance himself from philosophy's 'cool, contemporary style' – of which he is himself, in other contexts, one of the chief exponents. At any rate, I am of course naturally disposed to applaud his insistence on not letting high-faluting philo-sophical theory get the better of us, and on keeping ourselves in touch with 'what it is actually like' to be in relationships of various kinds.

Strawson's essay is centrally about free will, about freedom and responsibility. But one of his key ideas, as expressed in these words, is that it is a basic datum for us that our interactions with other persons are of a quite different kind from our interactions with anything else. What is it that makes the difference? Following some more recent philosophers, most notably Stephen Darwall, who have taken up the research programme that Strawson sketches in 'Freedom and Resentment', we may call it *second-personality*.

What is second-personality? To answer that, we may begin with Strawson's distinction between 'objective' and 'reactive' attitudes. Any interpersonal relationship worthy of the name, let alone any worth calling *love*, will necessarily involve a nexus of what Strawson calls reactive attitudes – gratitude, resentment, and the like – which characteristically involve my seeing and appraising, from my standpoint as a responsible being, the other person as someone who is simultaneously involved in so seeing and appraising *me*, from *her* standpoint as a responsible being.

Strawson's treatment of this theme in 'Freedom and Resentment' is likely to remind us, or at least those of us who have read around a bit in philosophy, of Paul Grice's (1957) thesis that linguistic meaning depends on recursively recognised intentions. Indeed Grice's work may well have been part of the background to Strawson's thinking. For

Strawson as for Grice, the idea is that reactive attitudes *reverberate*; they iterate, like a torch shining into a mirror set up opposite another mirror. That is how, for instance, it is when there are beliefs about beliefs, as in a famous line in Dante's *Inferno* (13.25): 'cred'io ch'ei credette ch'io credesse ...'; 'I think he thought I thought ...'.

It may also remind many of us of themes that are central to the work of Iris Murdoch, who (in her decidedly *un*cool, and not entirely conventional, style of doing philosophy) often comes out with remarks like the following:

> Love is knowledge of the individual.
> When M is just and loving she sees D as she really is.
> Love is the perception of individuals. Love is the extremely difficult realisation that something other than oneself is real. (1999, 321, 329, 215)

Strawson and Murdoch share a focus on the reality of people *as people*, people in just the same sense as I myself am a person. Together they give us the makings of a rich and perceptive account of any interpersonal relationship, including those that we would naturally describe in English as relationships of love or friendship. The account of love toward which Strawson and Murdoch are pointing us will be one that stresses the mutuality and interdependence of the persons involved in love, and the tendency of ideas and attitudes to 'reverberate' (as I put it) between them. Above all, in line with Strawson's main project of vindicating our pre-philosophical ideas of freedom and responsibility and Murdoch's main project of overcoming the 'fat relentless ego', it will be an account that stresses the absolutely bedrock difference, for us, between encountering another person, and encountering, say, a rock or a rubber plant.

It is this difference between reactive and objective attitudes, as Strawson calls them, that utilitarianism seems to fail to make good sense of, leading it to become (as I argued in Chapter 2) a fundamentally solipsistic philosophy to which *I and the world* are fundamental, but *you* (or *we*) are not: a philosophy for which, at bottom, *all* attitudes are objective (attitudes to objects) and none of them are reactive (attitudes to persons, as such). Utilitarianism is all about benevolence – about my attempts to make the world a better place. But benevolence is not enough for love, because love is essentially second-personal.

In Chapter 3, I characterised friendship as benevolent companionship over time. 'Love' and 'friendship' are English words that we use in obviously different ways; there are other kinds of love besides friendship, and 'love' is generally used of more intense relationships than 'friendship'. (More about some of the differences in Chapters 11 ff.). Still, it is part of the usefulness of this chapter's foray into the philosophy of love that it seems more or less right to use this same characterisation of love too. Friendship is benevolent companionship over time, and love too is benevolent companionship over time.

This means, as I said in discussing C. S. Lewis's notion of *agape* in Chapter 8, that there is more to love and friendship than simple benevolence, for both involve two further ingredients alongside benevolence. One of these further ingredients is picked out by the word 'companionship'; we can call it *second-personality*. The other is picked out by

111

'over time'; we can call it *loyalty*. A little about these two ingredients in turn.

Second-personality shows up in love and friendship like this: love and friendship are *I-involving* and *you-involving*. The benevolent person is, to use Strawson's adjective, 'cool': she just disinterestedly wants things to go well. But the loving person cares that *she* should make things go well *for you*. For Jane to love John is not merely for her to want his well-being in the neutral way in which we might press a voting-button. It is for Jane to want that *she should bring about* John's well-being in an engaged and affective sense of wanting, a sense which has *longing* for his well-being at one end of the spectrum, and being pained if he does not get it, in a way which is far from 'disinterested', at most points along the spectrum. As such, love involves the emotions (and the risk of negative emotions) in ways that benevolence never does.

If Jane feels straightforward benevolence toward John, it cannot (or should not) matter to her whether it is *Jane* who brings about John's well-being, just as long as he does well. It is not part of *benevolence* toward John to feel pain about his missed well-being, however 'regrettable' (in benevolence's cool vocabulary) missing that well-being might have been, and however 'desirable' (also a cool usage: here *desire* in any affective sense is precisely *not* in question) that particular instance of well-being may be. Here the concern is like that prompted by a ringing phone in the workplace: the concern is merely that *someone* should respond. To love, by contrast, it typically does matter that it should be *me* who responds. The idea of jealous benevolence, or of competition to be the one who does the good for John, is mildly absurd. The idea of jealous or competitive love is not absurd at all, but entirely familiar. In this sense the motivations of love recognise the import-ance of *my* involvement in what happens.

This I-involvingness and you-involvingness of love comes out in other ways too. For instance, when Jane loves John (again: not necessarily romantically), she wants to be with him; she wants her and John's minds to meet and their journeys to coincide. She wants John and herself to become an 'us', and she wants that us to share narratives, histories, a conversation, a trail of back-references and jokes and allu-sions. And (despite Emerson in Chapter 2) love, almost by definition and certainly by nature, demands reciprocity: what Jane wants concerning John, she wants John to want concerning her. Whereas there is nothing in the nature of benevolence that requires me to wish the object of my benevolence to wish me well back (unless of course I think that it will do him good to wish me well). Not only can I wish well-being on someone I have no positive desire to meet; I can wish well-being on people I hope to avoid entirely. Benevolence toward John and wanting to be *involved* with John are attitudes that float entirely free of each other.

This notion of 'becoming an us' brings us to the third ingredient of love, alongside benevolence and second-personality: loyalty or commitment.

It is not just that, *at* some time, John has Jane's just and truthful attention and her good will, and she his. It is also that, *over* time, Jane acts out of a disposition to keep things that way, and to keep them that way relative to John in particular. Jane makes and maintains a standing choice to go on giving John her care and attention, and to make him particularly, perhaps even exclusively, the object of her care and attention. Her commitment to him is *selective*: there are plenty of other people whom Jane could, in principle, have loved just as easily and just as much as she loves John. But *as things are*, it is *John* she loves (whatever kind of love we may be talking about – not necessarily romance). Given the facts about her and his past history, chosen or unchosen, the two of them are together now, and live in the light of that shared history. And that means that, beyond a certain point, he and she *simply do not attend* to the lovableness of other people than Jane (in John's case) or John (in Jane's).

Comparisons might be available. For any good quality that Jane loves in John, there might be plenty of other chaps out there who have more of it. But that is beside the point – and *they* are beside the point. For – to use two phrases that *do* go specifically with romantic love – Jane and John are simply 'not on the market'; they have 'eyes only for each other'. What do they see in each other? Part of what they see in each other is someone who isn't always asking what they see in each other: someone who is prepared to stop 'looking for an upgrade', and settle for the person they've got. Precisely because it is a key part of love to set aside just that sort of question, love is not just benevolence plus second-personality; it is those two things plus *loyalty* – selective and sometimes even exclusive commitment. And though romantic love is a more intense thing than friendship, these remarks apply to both these kinds of love:

114

friendship may not (usually) be such a deep or exclusive commitment as romantic love, but it too involves loyalty.

As Troy Jollimore has shown in his wonderful book *Love's Vision* (2011), there are aspects of this selectiveness that fail to have any rational justification, not because they are irrational or unjustified so much as because they simply fall outside the scope of rational justification. The choice to select one other person only to love is characteristic above all of romantic love (at least in societies where monogamy has a central place). But it is not absent in other kinds of love: think of a mother's devotion to her child, or of the *particular* place, even if it is a relatively small place, that any individual friend will occupy in your world. For Jane to devote herself to John's charms is, among other things, a choice *not to respond to* (at times, not even to *see*) the charms of other men. No doubt it is not hard to provide a second-order justification of this first-order decision to blind herself to other men's charms for the sake of John's, and of his parallel decision in Jane's favour. At the first order, though, it is a decision of a kind to be unresponsive to certain sorts of reason. As we might also put it – deploying a nice distinction of Kate Abramson and Adam Leite's (2011) – it is a decision to let the reasons *of* love trump the reasons *for* love. That is, it is a choice for Jane to act on the presently powerful reasons that *derive from* her relationship with John, rather than on the original reasons that *led her to* that relationship, such as John's being charming, funny, kind, brilliant at both ping-pong and modal logic, smoking-hot in bed, and whatever else originally drew, and with any luck still draws, a girl like her to a boy like him.

For Jane to love John is for her, to one degree or another – most strongly if, as let us suppose, John is her lover – to be exclusive about John. Because she loves John, Jane focuses on him in a way that she focuses on no one else. Now there are reasons why John originally became her lover, why he attracted her ('reasons *for* love', in Abramson and Leite's (2011) terminology), and with any luck they will still apply: she will still burn the same flame for him tonight that she did the night their relationship began. But this does not create a 'trading-up' problem. No doubt it is true that she loves (or began to love) John because he has (had) qualities ABC. And no doubt any Tom, Dick, or Harry might come along with a greater quantity of ABC than John has. Yet it is not the case that Jane would be rationally obliged, or even rationally warranted, in trading in John for Tom, Dick, or Harry, should she meet them. Jane might meet them and it might *not even cross her mind* to do a trade-in, or even a comparison of their good qualities with John's. And this is because 'reasons *of* love' – reasons arising from within Jane's continuing commitment to John – have the form and the force to silence those 'reasons *for* love' of other men than John.

For similar reasons, neither does Jane's commitment to John on the basis of the reasons provided by his qualities ABC mean that she thinks everyone else should love John the way she does. Nor does it mean that, if other people display the valuable properties ABC to a similar extent to John, Jane is rationally obliged – or even warranted – in loving them too, just to the extent that they too display ABC. Jane focuses *exclusively* on John, because she is *exclusively* committed to him. That exclusive commitment silences, or blinds Jane to, certain sorts of reasons.

(Here, as Jollimore (2011) points out, is a good philosophical reason for agreeing that 'love is blind' – at the same time as being a matter of *vision*.) This chosen unresponsiveness to reasons is, as we may say, arational. It is not an *ir*rational thing, but it is not a rational thing either. It's just a thing.

That is one way – deliberate selectiveness – in which love, including both friendship and romantic love, is arational. Another noteworthy way is *contingency*. If Jane and John's is a romantic love, then very likely – and setting aside the possibility of up-to-date dating agencies with complex couple-matching algorithms – it will be true to say that it was not a matter of rational calculation that they fell in love; they just did. They were not selected for each other, either by a website or by the guardians of some Platonic Republic; they just happened to meet. What is true here of marital love is, of course, even more obviously true of sibling love, or parent–child love, even of classmate friendship. By and large, we do not *pick* these relationships, *for reasons*. They just *come to* us: not irrationally, but certainly arationally, and – as I say – contingently.

The contingency of love, in this sense, can and should give us a certain sense of vertigo. If *love* is contingent – as we might well think, given its centrality in our lives – then everything is. Including, vertiginously enough, our own existence.

The Right Train
I've done some bad things and I've done some mad things.
I've done some things that got me in the stew.
Many of my options are not for sane adoption;

but I did a good thing when I married you.

Some people's choices are based on hearing voices.
Some read the stars, or the leaves in their Typhoo.
I treat life's junctions with minimal compunction;
but I took the right fork when I married you.

We have shared the sunlight, and the sudden-failed
    umbrella.
We have sat out winters that stormed out of the blue.
Warmth drives branches upwards; cold pushes roots
    deeper.
What would I have done, if I hadn't married you?

Life is all alternatives, but hopeless information.
Unmarked and unsignalled, and too many for clear view,
trains line every platform through the vastness of life's
    station;
but I caught the right train the day I married you.
                         (Chappell 2021, poem 28)

It is a matter of – very often – bare-headed chance that we
have the lovers, friends, and (of course) family that we do.
To some extent at least, we did not choose them; at most, as
particularly with lovers (in a liberal society with no arranged
marriages), we chose them from a range of possible alternatives that came our way pretty much by chance. (Even if we
tempered chance via a dating website, chance remains in the
mix.) We might say that our fortunes in affairs of love are a
matter of an *ethical trajectory*. We have lives going on, and
they are *journeys*. Our choices are not made, as is imagined
by some philosophers (including utilitarians again), on the
basis of what Jollimore (2011, 76 ff.) calls 'a comprehensive

comparative survey', or what I have criticised as the option-range conception of ethical choice (Chappell 2001): we do not stand *outside* life evaluating and comparing the values *inside* it, and no creature that did that would be remotely like *us*. We have little or no choice over what choices we make; here too we are subject to contingency, and indeed to risk.

That sums up my account of love as benevolent companionship over time. It gives us at least some idea of what the difference is between simple benevolence, wanting things to go well for someone, and actual love, which is benevolence *plus second-personality plus loyalty*. Everything I have just said about love as benevolent companionship over time is also, I want to suggest, equally true of friendship as benevolent companionship over time.

But now, we can no longer avoid a question that I have been carefully postponing. What is the difference between love and friendship? How are we to distinguish the two?

Well, to begin with, of course, we don't always need to distinguish the two. It is not wrong to say that friendship is a kind of love; so at least some love *just is* friendship. And if we don't use the word friendship of the other kinds of love, such as parent–child or romantic love, that may often seem little more than an accident of language. Still, there are some clear differences in the semantic range of the two terms, and some of these differences are even philosophically interesting. One of the main differences is that, as a rule, love is an emphatic good, and friendship is an unemphatic good. Let me begin to explain this difference in Chapter 11.

11 Friendship as an Unemphatic Good

I have been saying things about the philosophy of love at least some of which it wouldn't really do to say about the philosophy of friendship – even though some of them are true. Why wouldn't it do? Well, we come back here to a problem that I noted in the literature of the philosophy of friendship as far back as Chapter 2: as I called it there, po-facedness.

The all too frequent po-facedness of philosophy about friendship contrasts sharply with the un-po-facedness of friendship itself. In real life, our actual friendships are typically anything but high-minded or moralistic. They are much less likely to find their characteristic expression in earnest prayer meetings, pious mutual-admiration clubs, or gatherings aimed at mutual consciousness-raising than in games of tennis, sharing a library table, or having a quiet meal together. Except where it is distorted by ideology – in the way that, for example, evangelical Christianity can unfortunately tend to reduce friendships to a means to Getting People Saved – friendship as we actually experience it is, as I shall put it, typically an *unemphatic good*. And philosophers seem characteristically prone to miss this point.

Not of course that it is only philosophers' accounts of friendship that go off the rails in this direction of over-earnestness. (Recall methodological notes #1 and #2 from

Chapter 1.) There are also plentiful examples in stories and novels that suggest that literary treatments of friendship are not at their best, either, when they are self-conscious and emphatic – or when the friendships they describe are self-conscious and emphatic. Putting an overdone friendship in a novel can be a quick way to ruin the book.

One book that illustrates this very well – I mentioned it in passing in Chapter 1 – is the best-known school novel of the nineteenth century, Thomas Hughes' manifesto for 'muscular Christianity', *Tom Brown's Schooldays* (1857). In that book we may usefully contrast the main character's two best friends: the amusing and mischievous scamp Harry East on the one side, and on the other, George Arthur. Hughes himself tells us that Arthur is 'delicate' and 'scholarly'. Many readers will quickly conclude that what George Arthur turns out to be, quite unlike either Tom or Harry, is sickly and priggish. Another famous fictional English schoolboy, Nigel Molesworth, would certainly have dismissed Arthur in short order, as 'uterly wet and a wede' (Whillans and Searle 1954). (Indeed: modulo the differences between the sentimental mode and the comic, the striking resemblance between *Tom Brown*'s George Arthur and *How to Be Topp*'s Basil Fotherington-Thomas is surely no coincidence.)

Harry East only wants to go bird's-nesting with Tom Brown, and help him fight off the bullies like Flashman who infest the chaotic jungle of their school. But Arthur wants Tom and himself to have Serious Talks, and to read the Bible together.

However laudable such earnest and pious aims might be, they do nothing at all, aesthetically speaking, for

121

Tom Brown the novel. It is arguable that they do not do much either, ethically speaking, for Tom Brown the boy. When Arthur arrives, no doubt Hughes' muscular-Christian novel gets more Christian, but it also gets strikingly less muscular. Gone is the healthy and at times rather hair-raisingly brutal fresh-air realism, the whiff both of *Jorrocks* and of a junior-school *Tom Jones*, that is the dominating tone of the early chapters of *Tom Brown*. This red-faced Berkshire-squire heartiness is increasingly replaced by a tone of suffocatingly pious melodrama, culminating in passionate protestations of affection in a near-deathbed scene of just the kind that most modern readers are more likely to find ridiculous than tear-jerking. (Oscar Wilde on Dickens' *Old Curiosity Shop*: 'It would take a heart of stone to read the death of Little Nell without laughing.')

By the end of the book, all has become Victorian in the very worst sense of the word. And through his relationship with Arthur, Tom loses realism too. Whereas before he was a happy mischievous mongrel, capering off the leash through the Out-of-Bounds of the vasty fields of 1830s Warwickshire, now Tom is a poodle walking on its hind legs; he becomes a rather strained and puzzled apprentice-prig, led by the nose by Arthur's sermonising in a way that is much too far from what is natural for him, or anyone, to count as 'an improvement in his character' at all. Of course Tom – and Harry too – certainly need to become maturer, more reflective, steadier beings; they are, after all, rough teenage boys in a rough society. Still, their sentimental education via Arthur seems more than a little forced and, well, sentimental. Here too, as much as from philosophy, the lesson to draw is that friendship is at its best when it is neither forced nor given to moralistic prosing. Because friendship is an unemphatic good.

It is easy for a philosopher to write about friendship; it is very hard for a philosopher to write well about friendship. (As, by this point, the reader may be feeling they know to their cost.) The natures of the two things rub against each other. Friendship is contentment; philosophy is discontent. Philosophy is intense; friendship is laid-back. Philosophy doubts; friendship takes for granted. Philosophy anxiously seeks reassurance and certainty about what no one normally questions; friendship basks unanxiously in what it is happily confident of. The whole point of philosophy, as very often practised, is to set up reasons to question and distrust, then to build systems of thought that will – supposedly – overcome the distrust. The whole point of friendship, as usually experienced, is to be unsystematic and free, and to rest relaxedly on unexplored and untheorised mutual confidence.

Friendship goes unspoken; philosophy says everything (which is, according to Voltaire, the secret to being a bore). Philosophy is about 'making it explicit'; friendship is about tacit shared assumption. Philosophy writes in black and white, and as clearly and starkly as possible; friendship – like happiness, according to the French writer Henry de Montherlant – 'writes white'. Whatever it takes as its topic, philosophy makes that topic into something focal and sharp-edged, right in the middle of our field of attention. But most friendship, most of the time, is peripheral not focal to our attention, and proceeds on terms that are implicit and assumed, not sharply focused or explicitly defined.

Like the air we breathe and the light that we see by and the water we drink and the earth we tread, friendship is, for most of us, a very great good in our lives. But usually friendship is, like those elemental realities, an *unemphatic* good. It isn't a good that we naturally focus our attention on, and it isn't normally a good that we 'get heavy about' or make a great deal of fuss over. Whereas philosophy is *all about* focused, concentrated attention on whatever it takes as its topic. (And, you may be tempted to add, philosophy is all about making a fuss.)

We see the unemphaticness of friendship in real life, and we see it in the books we read and the plays and films we watch. Alexander Nehamas, in his classic book *On Friendship*, notices and discusses how rarely we encounter great stories that are centrally about friendship: 'Here is a curious fact – unexpected and startling to me when I first became aware of it: I was struck by how rare it is to find a novel of the first rank that takes friendship as its central subject' (2016, 82). Nehamas himself can think of no clearer example of a famous novel about friendship than *Huckleberry Finn*. But even this example is a bit dubious; even there, as he notes, 'Twain focuses his gaze more on Huck's recognition that this black man is as fully human as he is himself, and less on his characters' friendship in its own right' (2016, 82–83). 'Nothing is more central to [any] novel,' Nehamas goes on to note more generally (2016, 86–87), 'than the depiction of intimate human relationships'. Yet 'despite the immense weight of the epic tradition that associates friendship with extreme situations and extraordinarily passionate feelings . . . friendship in modern times has become, for better or worse, a milder affair.'

124

Actually, I think the contrast that Nehamas wishes to draw here between friendship in 'the epic tradition' and in 'modern times' does not exist either. Both in ancient times and in modern, typical friendships have usually been unemphatic. What is most immediately striking, for instance, about the Greek dramatists' various depictions of Orestes' best and most loyal friend Pylades, is that Pylades never says a word. Even the greatest case of a friend of all in ancient literature, Achilles' friend Patroclus in the *Iliad*, only comes to life as a character (and a hero) in his own right when he is *not with Achilles*. Conversely, Achilles only comes back into the forefront of the *Iliad*'s action once (and indeed because) Patroclus himself has been killed, and Achilles feels a need to avenge Patroclus' death by killing his killer, Hector. The passages of the *Iliad* where Achilles and Patroclus are together are remarkably few, and mostly remarkably short. And even when they are presented together, their friendship is hardly ever the main focus, either of Homer's art or of their attention.

This is most obvious of all in the longest depiction of the two of them together, which is just over 500 lines long, in *Iliad* Book 9.182–712, when the other Greek generals come to their tent to plead with Achilles to return to help them in their faltering war against Troy. Throughout this long and vivid debate Patroclus says nothing at all; he is completely silent. At line 190 he is even introduced as 'the silent Patroclus'. Here is part of the passage, in my own translation:

185   The heralds arrived at Achilles' men's camp and ships,
       and came on the hero, Achilles himself, at rest,
       taking delight in the sweet voice of a lyre,

> fine-made and ornate, and silver-bridged
> (spoil it was from the sack of Eetion's town);
> he played for his pleasure, singing of men's great deeds.
> 190   He was alone except for the silent Patroclus,
> who sat and watched the singing of Achilles,
> speaking no word till the recitation was done ...

Actually Patroclus still 'speaks no word' after the recitation ends, either. Not at least any words that Homer records, and nothing to anyone except Achilles' servants, to whom he is, throughout Book 9, no more than Achilles' butler-in-chief. Both for Achilles and Patroclus in the poem, and for Homer outside it, their friendship is not a focus, a point of emphasis. It is an *assumed background* to what is focused on and emphasised. The moral is clear, I think: despite what Nehamas says, it is as true of ancient literature as it is of modern that friendships in literature are typically, and especially under favourable conditions, an unemphatic good.

Another classic example of friendship as an unemphatic good, this time from a century much closer to our own, comes in Jane Austen's *Pride and Prejudice* (1813). The friendship between the sisters Jane and Lizzy Bennet is deeply felt; most certainly we can call it love. And their friendship is a fact of foundational importance to them both, especially given how unreliable everyone else is in their family. Yet *Pride and Prejudice* is not a novel about Jane and Lizzy's friendship, any more than it is a novel about the house the Bennets live in. Rather like that house, their friendship is not so much the plot as a precondition of the plot. (And at some points in the story, both their friendship and their family house seem under threat. These threats are part of the story, but they do not make either the friendship or the house the star of the novel.)

Or consider – if only for the sake of its title – Charles Dickens' *Our Mutual Friend* (1865). Among other things, this is a novel about two lawyers who are friends, Eugene Wrayburn and Mortimer Lightwood. Their friendship is important – by the end of the novel, very important – both to Wrayburn and Lightwood, and to the shape of the novel that they are in. Yet *Our Mutual Friend* is not a novel about their friendship. Nor, despite its name, is it mainly a novel about any other friendship, either. It is a novel not about friendship, but about love and money. The novel runs two separate love stories, and four or five distinct narratives about the corrupting power of wealth (and indeed poverty). The links between its various settings and narrative lines are established by a number of threads of mutual friendship. But these mutual friendships, the two lawyers' among them, constitute the novel's narrative background – not its foreground.

Wrayburn and Lightwood's friendship perhaps comes closest to being focal when, late on in the book, Dickens indulges in another instance of that stock-in-trade of Victorian authors, a near-deathbed scene. As I remarked above, such things are no longer very much to our taste, at least not if handled as Dickens' age was wont to handle them. But Eugene's case is a good deal less embarrassingly overdone, and a good deal less narratively gratuitous, than Arthur's in *Tom Brown's Schooldays*; if it leads to protestations of love from the apparently dying Eugene, these are not, you will perhaps be relieved to hear, mainly about his love for Mortimer.

Another fictional friendship that is mostly non-focal and unemphatic is found in perhaps the most famous play in the world, Shakespeare's *Hamlet*. Hamlet's best friend is Horatio. In a society of sinisterly heavy surveillance ('Denmark's a prison') Horatio is Hamlet's only reliable confidant, and Horatio is the only person of Hamlet's own social class who also sees the Ghost. With almost his last words (yes, another deathbed scene, though in this case the 'bed' is the floor, splashed with blood and poisoned wine, of the banqueting hall in Elsinore Castle), Hamlet begs Horatio to tell his story after he has died. Their friendship is important to them, and to the play. Yet *Hamlet* is not a play about Horatio and Hamlet's friendship. And it would be a completely different, and probably lesser, play if it was. As indeed Hamlet himself famously seems to suggest, abruptly curtailing one of the few speeches where he actually becomes emphatic about his friendship with Horatio, even though what he is saying is precisely that we should not be *too* emphatic in friendship:

> Give me that man
> That is not passion's slave, and I will wear him
> In my heart's core, ay, in my heart of heart,
> As I do thee. – Something too much of this. (3.2.71–74)

Or what about Sherlock Holmes and Dr John Watson – either in any of the various TV and film versions, or in the original books of stories? At the simple level of plot construction, Watson is needed because, like so many fictional detectives since, Sherlock needs someone to explain things to. (Perhaps, come to think of it, Hamlet needs Horatio for a similar reason, and Lizzy Bennet needs Jane, and Wrayburn and Lightwood need each other ... This is also, of course, why Dr Who always has a companion.) Does Sherlock need Watson *within* the story, or does Watson need Sherlock? Probably. But it would be most unlike either of them to *admit* to this need. What they focus on together is solving unsolved crimes. For either of them, and particularly Sherlock, to admit even that he is fond of the other takes some doing. For either of them to admit to *needing* the other would be undignified and embarrassing inside the story, and a kind of disappointment to the reader outside the story. Such outbursts of explicit emotion – such fussing and gassing, as Dr Watson himself might call it – would 'let the side down'. They would be out of character both for a clubbable gentleman doctor with a background in the Indian Army, and for a rather reclusive misanthrope of undoubted genius but uncertain origin.

It seems to be a general truth about friendships like these that they only become focal, or central, or get directly concentrated upon, *when things go wrong*. The whole pleasure and point of a friendship of this kind is just to swing along as usual, simply enjoying the steady and happy condition of friendship without ever needing to fuss or gas, or to pry very much into its psychological foundations. (Peter Pan to Wendy, in the 2003 film, when she is led by her more-than-friendly feelings towards Peter to pry in this way: 'We have fun together, don't we? Why do you always spoil it?') Holmes and Watson; Wrayburn and Lightwood; even the femininely stereotyped, and therefore more naturally 'gushing', Jane and Lizzy are not easily pushed into any kind of effusive protestation of friendship unless some crisis comes to hand – though, given that they are all characters in novels, crises there are quite certain to be. (Even more so in a revenger's tragedy like *Hamlet*.)

For sure, when friends are in a corner or a crisis, they will look out for each other, support each other, make sacrifices for each other – maybe even die for one other (or in Achilles' case, kill). Or when a friend goes off the rails, his real friends will show their true quality by trying to get him *back* on the rails – as Mole, Badger, and Ratty do for Mr Toad in *The Wind in the Willows* (Grahame 1908). That does not mean that friendship is most clearly and characteristically expressed in such extreme and emphatic actions. Maybe we should say that, on the contrary, friendship is most clearly and characteristically expressed in things like playing music for each other, or watching a silly film together, or in a fireside game of dominoes in a quiet corner of the pub – or as Ratty puts it in *The Wind in the Willows*, in 'messing about in boats'. The desperate and daring deeds that friendship certainly *sometimes* involves are not even needed until things have already gone pretty badly wrong.

'Greater love hath no man than this', Jesus says in John 15.13 (and our last aphorism), 'that he lay down his life for his friends.' Well, for sure that is the most *extreme* thing that a friend's love can do. But much of the time the whole point of friendship is not to be in an extreme at all, but in a steady state, a 'sabbath rest by Galilee', as indeed Jesus comes close to saying to Martha with his 'One thing is needful' at Luke 10.42.

Most of the time the whole point and pleasure of friendship is that it is neither extreme, nor emphatic. Most of the time friendship can exist, and get along very well indeed, without even being explicitly mentioned. As all these and plenty of other literary examples suggest, friendship is not at its best when we focus upon it, when we make it self-conscious, or when we make a fuss about it. And as the long and happily married will tell you: over time, this lack of fuss becomes one of the best things even about the supposedly ultra-emphatic friendship that is marriage.

So friendship is best enjoyed as an unemphatic good. And next is a real-life story that illustrates the point further.

12   Bertrand Russell and His
Over-Emphatic 'German' Friend

In the autumn term of 1911, the relatively equable and straightforward Bertrand Russell (who was thirty-nine at the time) began a friendship with a strange and wild-eyed foreigner, a twenty-two-year-old Manchester University engineering student, who began to show up repeatedly at Russell's door in Staircase I of Nevile's Court, Trinity College Cambridge. '[C. K. Ogden and I] were in the middle of . . . a lot of complicated problems [in mathematical logic] when an unknown German appeared, speaking very little English but refusing to speak German . . .' (Russell, letter to Lady Ottoline Morrell, 18 October 1911, in McGuinness 1988, 89).

This amiable lack of extremity that I have been talking about, this happy swinging-along without crises or emergencies or pompous cant or fuss, is no doubt exactly what Russell hoped for from their friendship. But whatever else he may have got from it, Russell never got *that*. The 'unknown German' (actually he was an Austrian, though he often referred to himself as a German) quickly became a most persistent and not altogether considerate visitor. The very next day Russell was writing to his long-term mistress and principal confidante Ottoline Morrell that 'my German friend threatens to be an infliction' (19 October), and only a week later that 'my German, who seems to be rather good, was very argumentative' (25 October) and even 'tiresome'

(1 November). Russell doubted initially whether his visitor was 'a man of genius or a crank' (McGuinness 1988, 89), and so apparently did the visitor himself. As Russell later retold the anecdote for BBC Radio 4's 'Great Lives' series:

> He was queer [as in 'strange'], and his notions seemed to me odd, so that for a whole term I could not make up my mind whether he was a man of genius or merely an eccentric. At the end of his first term at Cambridge he came to see me and said 'Will you please tell me whether I am a complete idiot or not? If I am a complete idiot I shall become an aeronaut, but if I am not I shall become a philosopher.' I told him to write me something during the vacation on some philosophical subject, and I would then tell him whether he was a complete idiot or not. At the beginning of the following term he brought me the fulfilment of this suggestion. After reading only one sentence I said to him 'No! You must not become an aeronaut!' (http://www.bbc.co.uk/programmes/b0184rgn)

And so Russell's encouragement set in train the career of the greatest philosopher of the twentieth century, Ludwig Wittgenstein. It also began a friendship that changed the course of both their lives. Though sadly, the two of them fairly definitely outlived their friendship, and even while it endured, it was always fluctuating wildly, always coming and going.

It was not long after Russell first realised Wittgenstein's extraordinary talent that he was prepared to tell Ottoline 'I really like him very much' (McGuinness 1988, 98), and even that 'I love him' (Monk 1990, 41). That Wittgenstein reciprocated this affection was quite evident to Russell ('I think he is passionately devoted to me', McGuinness 1988, 102) and also, very clearly, to Wittgenstein himself. But even in the most favourable phase of their friendship, from 1911 to 1914 (when the war left them on opposites sides and in different and hostile countries), it was consistently stormy.

Though both of these brilliant men were naturally analytical and talkative, indeed argumentative, these storms came largely from a single source: from Wittgenstein's very difficult personality, and in particular from his inability ever to stop torturously analysing himself, his relationship with Russell, and everything else around him. By Russell's own account, Wittgenstein would appear uninvited at Russell's door in Trinity very late at night, then stay for hours, either talking non-stop about logic or, even more tryingly, saying nothing at all. In his *Autobiography* Russell remarks – with an only slightly unconvincing bravado – that going to prison for his pacificism in 1918 was 'quite agreeable', because 'I had no engagements, no difficult decisions to make, no fear of callers, no interruptions to my work' (1967, 256). Are these last two phrases in particular a hint, perhaps, that it was Wittgenstein's calls and interruptions that Russell had particularly dreaded 'outside'?

> He strains his mind to the utmost constantly, at things which are discouraging by their difficulty, and nervous fatigue tells on him sooner or later . . . I told Wittgenstein yesterday that he thinks too much about himself, and if he begins again I shall refuse to listen unless I think he is quite desperate. He has talked it out now as much as is good for him. (McGuinness 1988, 154–155)

> He used to come to see me every evening at midnight, and pace up and down my room like a wild beast in agitated silence ... Once I said to him, 'Are you thinking about logic, or about your sins?' 'Both,' he replied, and continued his pacing. I did not like to suggest that it was time for bed, as it seemed probable both to him and me that on leaving me he would commit suicide. (McGuinness 1988, 155–156)

What Russell would have liked was simply a clever friend to talk logic with. What he got was a tormented genius who could not learn to leave well enough alone in any aspect of his life, including their friendship.

> I had an awful time with Wittgenstein yesterday between tea and dinner. He came analysing all that goes wrong between him and me and I told him I thought it was only nerves on both sides and everything was all right at bottom. Then he said he never knew whether I was speaking the truth or being polite, so I got vexed and refused to say another word. He went on and on. I sat down at my table and took up my pen and began to look through a book, but he still went on. At last I said sharply 'All you want is a little self-control.' Then at last he went away with an air of high tragedy ... (Monk 1990, 80)

After terrific quarrels, and much surely quite unnecessary pain and offence on both sides, the end of the main part of this friendship was characteristic of both men. And it is interesting to consider how and when friendships turn into enmities, or fail, or lose momentum, or just peter out. (We come back here to a question that I mentioned in Chapter 1: when is it right to end a friendship?)

In January 2014, after another exhausting alterca-
tion, Russell wrote to Wittgenstein simply asking him to
'behave as if nothing had happened'. But Wittgenstein
replied – at a length that I will not tax the reader's patience
with – in a letter that began like this:

> I can't possibly carry out your request . . . that would go
> clean contrary to my nature. So *forgive me for this long
> letter* and remember that I *have to* follow my own nature
> just as much as you. During the last week I have thought
> a lot about our relationship and I have come to the
> conclusion that we really don't suit one another. *This is
> not meant as a reproach!* – Either for you or for me. But it
> is a fact . . . (McGuinness 1988, 194; italics in original)

Wittgenstein finally concluded his letter with these words:

> *I shall be grateful to you and devoted to you for the rest of
> my life, but I shall not write to you again and you will not
> see me either.* Now that I am once again reconciled with
> you I want to part from you *in peace* so that we shan't
> some time get annoyed with one another again and then
> perhaps part as enemies. I wish you everything of the best
> and I beg you not to forget me and to think of me often
> *with friendly feelings.* Goodbye! (McGuinness 1988, 195;
> italics in original)

Despite Wittgenstein's melodramatic tone, this was not their
last ever communication, not by a long way. It was not in
fact *the* end, but it was *an* end: as McGuinness puts it (1988,
196), 'The quarrel was made up but the friendship was
ended; Wittgenstein would no longer bare his heart to
Russell.' What then had ended it if not, at least in part,

Wittgenstein's nervous and anxious insistence on constantly tugging up the roots of that friendship to inspect them?

At any rate their later attitudes to each other were never as friendly, and at times were positively testy. Some years after Wittgenstein's death, Russell remarked that 'the later Wittgenstein [. . .] seems to have grown tired of serious thinking and to have invented a doctrine which would make such an activity unnecessary' (Russell 1959, 161). And Wittgenstein was no less waspish about Russell: 'Russell's books should be bound in two colours, those dealing with mathematical logic in red – and all students of philosophy should read them; those dealing with ethics and politics in blue – and no one should be allowed to read them' (Monk 1990, 278). By the time he said this, Wittgenstein himself had famously become the public proponent of a two-part philosophy. This was a view that he was already developing in the spring of 1914, a philosophy that he wrote down in a book, the *Tractatus Logico-Philosophicus*, that 'comes in two parts' (as he put it in a famous letter to Ludwig Ficker in September or October 1919):

> . . . the one presented here plus all that I have not written. And it is precisely this second part that is the important one. My book draws limits to the sphere of the ethical from the inside as it were, and I am convinced that this is the ONLY rigorous way of drawing those limits. In short, I believe that where many others today are just gassing, I have managed in my book to put everything firmly in place by being silent about it . . . (Wittgenstein 1971, 16)

Everything that is genuinely sayable is scientific and not evaluative; everything that is evaluative is unsayable. When we look over the unhappy chronicle of Wittgenstein's friendship with Russell, and some of his other friendships too, and when we recall what I have been saying about friendship as an unemphatic good, it is rather tempting to conclude that those friendships might have gone a lot better if Wittgenstein had simply managed to say less. And many of us will add to ourselves, a little ruefully, that it's not only Wittgenstein that this is true of.

What went wrong between Wittgenstein and Russell was precisely their, and specifically Wittgenstein's, failure to respect in practice the key point that friendship is an unemphatic good, which flourishes best when we don't make a big song and dance about it. So maybe it is just the fact that friendship is an unemphatic good that also makes it hard for us philosophers to write about it – or at least, to write *well* about it. Indeed, bearing in mind the famous last line of Wittgenstein's *Tractatus* – 'What we cannot speak of we must pass over in silence' (1921, section 7) – maybe we would even do better not to write about friendship at all?

Well, by this stage of my own book about friendship, it's a bit late for that. And in any case I wouldn't go *that* far. I don't want to follow the Wittgenstein of the *Tractatus* all the way here. I don't agree with him that there is literally nothing that philosophers can meaningfully say about the value of anything, including unemphatic goods – and so, nothing meaningful to say about the value of friendship. Of course I think that there are things that it is worthwhile to say about the value of friendship. After all, here I am saying them. But there is something that I do want to agree with Wittgenstein about (at least in his theory, not his practice). It is this: there is something *elusive* about the concept of friendship, and about the ethics of friendship.

This elusiveness comes out in three further parameters for good philosophy about friendship. First, it needs to be *sensitive to tacit knowledge*; secondly, it needs to recognise the importance of *innocence*; and thirdly, it needs to avoid *moralism*. In different ways, these three further parameters are all, to some extent, already implicit in my discussion, and all have something to do with the unemphaticness of friendship.

I take the three parameters in turn in the next three chapters.

13 Sensitivity to Tacit Knowledge

T he phrase 'tacit knowledge' is normally connected with the work of the Hungarian-British scientist and philosopher Michael Polanyi (1888–1976). Polanyi's (1958) slogan in philosophy was 'We know more than we can tell'; 'tacit knowledge' was Polanyi's name for all the things that we know but *cannot* tell.

Polanyi's (1958) own examples of tacit knowledge include many cases of what philosophers often now call *practical* knowledge: knowing how to ride a bike, for instance, or the way that an apprentice carpenter may pick up good technique for making dovetail joints not by asking the master carpenter to explain them to her, but simply by watching and copying. In cases like these, not being able to explain in words what we want to teach isn't necessarily just our inarticulacy. What is to be taught is a skill or a craft or a disposition, and these things involve a kind of understanding that we might say 'outstrips words' – or, we might also say, never gets as far as words. I mean the kind of understanding that is involved, for instance, in seeing how to reconcile with each other the demands of two different roles both of which I occupy: *phronesis*, or 'judgement', as philosophers often call it (cp. Chapter 1).

It is also very often true that learning a craft or skill involves learning to follow a rule. And while there can be rules about how to follow rules (lawyers often formulate this kind of meta-rule), there can't be an infinite regress of rules about how to follow rules about how to follow rules about ... At some point we just have to get on and follow the rule without any further guidance. As Ludwig Wittgenstein (again) puts it in the late notebook that has been published as *On Certainty* (1969, paragraph 219), at some point we have to 'obey the rule *blindly*'. Doing this successfully involves another kind of tacit knowledge. It also, and connectedly, involves a disposition that we may call *spontaneity*.

Spontaneity means just doing what comes naturally. Provided what comes naturally to us is good, spontaneity is a good disposition for us to have (that is: it is a *virtue*). We aren't always spontaneous, nor should we be, but sometimes we should. Most of us have a reasonable knowledge of when it is a good idea to act in a pre-planned manner, and when it is a good idea to be spontaneous. But we can't be spontaneous by *planning* to be spontaneous, or by giving ourselves the command: 'Be spontaneous!' Being spontaneous by explicit plan, or in response to an explicit command, is not being spontaneous at all. So although we know when to be spontaneous, we don't normally make that knowledge explicit in our own practical reasoning. And we not only *don't* make it explicit; we *can't* make it explicit, because making it explicit would be self-defeating. If we made our knowledge of when to be spontaneous explicit in our practical reasoning, then spontaneity would become impossible for us – which it clearly isn't. So at least some of our knowledge of when to be spontaneous, and when not to be, has got to be tacit knowledge.

Spontaneity isn't the only valuable disposition, or virtue, to which something like this pattern of reasoning applies. For instance, it is generally a virtue for someone to be unselfconscious; maybe, too, unselfconsciousness is involved in quite a range of other virtues. (So, for instance, Aristotle connects it with generosity: 'It is the mark of the generous man that he does not consider himself', *Nicomachean Ethics* 1120b5–6.) But first, I cannot self-consciously cultivate my own virtue of unselfconsciousness. No doubt there are *some* ways for us to cultivate unselfconsciousness, and it would be interesting to think about what they might be. But whatever they are, they can't be direct and self-conscious methods, because self-conscious efforts to be unselfconscious are plainly and necessarily self-defeating.

Secondly, there are cases where what is needed is not the virtue of unselfconsciousness, but a different virtue: self-awareness or self-examination. For sure, good people have an understanding of which of these alternatives is appropriate in any particular situation. But as with spontaneity: whatever that understanding involves, it can't involve nothing but explicit knowledge. Because then it would involve the self-conscious thought 'Now I should be unselfconscious' – and that thought too involves a kind of self-defeat.

So unselfconsciousness is a second virtue, alongside spontaneity, that involves necessarily tacit knowledge. A third case is humility. Consider the question 'Will a genuinely humble person know that she is humble?' Some philosophers, for example Julia Driver (1989), have argued that the answer to this question has to be 'No'. If someone humble comes to believe that she is humble, then just by coming to believe that, she *ceases* to be humble. As Dickens' famously odious character Uriah Heep seems scripted to bring out, to think or say 'I am humble' is itself an act of pride. So that being humble is not something that I can *know*. For as soon as I believe it, my belief isn't true, and therefore isn't knowledge.

For my own part, I wouldn't go as far as Driver. I would want to distinguish the humble person *in a reflective moment* from the humble person *in action*. I agree that it is antithetical to humility to be thinking about how humble you are while acting humbly; that is what is wrong with Uriah Heep. But when you are not acting but sitting down and reflecting on your own character, I don't think that it is impossible for you to think, and think truly and aptly, 'Well, I may not have all the virtues, but at any rate I am humble.' Indeed, in a moment of reflection like that, you might also think truly (and aptly), 'I am unselfconscious' and 'I am spontaneous'. True, there would be something objectionably self-absorbed about someone who spent *a lot of time* reflecting on their own virtues in this way. But provided you don't get too self-absorbed, there is nothing impossible about thinking such things offline. The only thing that is impossible is to *act* humbly – or unselfconsciously or spontaneously – with your attention firmly fixed on your own virtues.

I say that spontaneity, unselfconsciousness, and humility are three examples of important valuable dispositions, virtues, that crucially involve tacit knowledge. And I say that friendship involves tacit knowledge too. Why and how?

Well, friendship involves tacit knowledge because (as should be obvious from the discussion above) friendship involves spontaneity, unselfconsciousness, and humility – so friendship inherits *their* commitments to tacit knowledge.

So friendship involves tacit knowledge because a lot of the time, being a good friend to someone involves not thinking directly and explicitly about what is involved in being a good friend to them. Suppose my friend Jane comes round to my house late at night crying her eyes out. What do I do? At once I put the kettle on, sit her down, hold her hand, and wait for her to be ready to tell me what's the matter. Do I act on a rule when I do this? Well, I might act in conformity with a rule, but that is a matter of correlation, not causation; it isn't the rule that makes me act like this. For I don't have to *work out* or *deduce* that this is the right thing to do. I don't need to do a little sum of practical reasoning in my head: 'Let me see, now – Jane is upset; I am Jane's friend; I should do what a friend will do for Jane when she is upset, and that is . . .' *I just do it*, without any conscious reasoning or deliberating at all; I just know that it's the right thing to do. And this knowledge is tacit knowledge, which I don't have to make explicit to know what is right to do, and to do it. What's more, I would be much less of a friend to Jane if I *did* have to work it out. The more I have to reason out what friendship involves, the less I seem to *understand* what friendship involves. Such reasoning looks like a bad case of what philosophers sometimes call, following Bernard Williams (1981, 18), 'a thought too many'.

Friendship, then, involves tacit knowledge both in its own right, and also because friendship involves the virtues of spontaneity, unselfconsciousness, and humility, and inherits their involvement with tacit knowledge. So if philosophers want to write well about friendship, they will have to do justice to the role of tacit knowledge in it.

14   Innocence

Alongside the involvement of friendship with spontaneity, unselfconsciousness, and humility, friendship also involves at least one other virtue that necessarily involves tacit knowledge. I shall call this virtue *innocence*.

Innocence is an interesting and difficult concept. In rather the same way as humility, spontaneity, and unselfconsciousness, its difficulties have to do with the familiar idea of 'thinking the unthinkable'. Innocence, in brief, is the virtue of *not* thinking the unthinkable – of having the tacit knowledge that enables you to avoid even thinking about what it is better not even to think about.

To see that innocence in this meaning of the word is indeed a virtue, consider some further words from Bernard Williams:

> One does not feel easy with the man who in the course of a discussion of how to deal with political or business rivals says, 'Of course, we could have them killed, but we should lay that aside right from the beginning.' It should never have come into his hands to be laid aside. It is characteristic of morality that it tends to overlook the possibility that some concerns are best embodied ... in deliberative silence. (1985, 206)

The central idea of the virtue of innocence is this: that for some possible thoughts about what to do, it is the mark of the good person, not that she will impassively review them as possible alternatives along with all the others, and then dutifully reject them in line with morality, but that she will never have those thoughts in the first place.

As I have pointed out elsewhere (Chappell 2022a), there are plenty of horrendously nasty things that you could be doing right now that you don't even need to reject as possibilities for action, because they simply haven't occurred to you, because you are not (I trust) a maniac. Suppose, for example, that you ask me, 'What shall we do this afternoon?' 'Well', I musingly reply, 'We could burn some puppies to death; or we could drown Grandma in the creek; or we could go into town with dirty needles and infect strangers with AIDS; or we could blow ourselves up committing a terrorist atrocity; or we could go for a walk in the park.' Being good at calculating consequences, we see straight off that going for a walk in the park is our best option from these alternatives.

I believe it is a central problem with a lot of contemporary moral philosophy that it seems committed to saying of this case that there is absolutely nothing wrong with our deliberation as I have just described it, just so long as that deliberation results in a good decision (and I have stipulated that it does). For a lot of contemporary moral philosophy, it seems that there would be absolutely nothing wrong with you or me as a deliberator if stuff like this happened all the time.

But suppose I do always consider puppy-burning as one of my alternatives, in every piece of deliberation that I ever perform. If no puppies or matches or petrol are readily available, my thoughts turn at once to the question how to procure some; when I am making what for most people is a two-way choice in the Breakfast Preserves aisle, the option of nipping out of the supermarket to torch a few baby spaniels is always there for me, alongside jam and marmalade, as a *third* possibility.

Now suppose that I share all my deliberating with you. Is it not even slightly likely that you will start to think that I am not quite a normal deliberator? Is there not even a small chance that you will be at first uneasy in my company – wondering if I am labouring a bad-taste running joke or something – then increasingly angry with me, and finally appalled at what you have come to think is a none-too-well-buried sadistic obsession of mine?

Here quite a few contemporary moral philosophers seem likely to say: 'Relax, everything's fine. Sophie Grace chooses jam and the walk in the park and the rest of it. She never *actually* burns any puppies. And puppy-burning is a really bad option, so pretty certainly she never will.' Is that how a *normal* person will respond? I don't think so. What a normal person will say, if I keep banging on about burning puppies sufficiently insistently – and even if I never actually burn any – is: 'Enough. This is disgusting. I don't wish to spend time with her. She shows a corrupt mind.'

Our character is shown, not only in what alternatives we *take*, but also in what alternatives we *take seriously*. Even to deliberate about some options – indeed even to have them occur to you – is evidence of a mind that lacks the virtue of innocence. It is not actually terribly nice to be made to consider the option of puppy-burning at all. (So I apologise to my readers for forcing it on them, and thereby threatening *their* innocence.)

Someone who is characteristically *not* like this about some range of possible atrocities, but on the contrary doesn't even consider them, is, we may say, innocent with respect to those atrocities. As we may also say, she has tacit knowledge that those things are not to be done. And the point that I am drawing from Williams, as cited above, is that this sort of tacit knowledge is, in general, good. It is, in general, a virtue to be innocent with respect to the vast majority of possible atrocities. For most of the horrendously nasty things that we could do, it is a mark of virtue in us if those possibilities never even occur to us – if our knowledge that those things are not to be done remains steadfastly tacit, or if, should they occur to us as bare possibilities, we mostly push them away with revulsion rather than allowing them to become serious possibilities.

The trouble is, of course, that I say 'most' and 'mostly' and 'in general'. If there are things that we should *generally* not even consider doing, then the typical philosopher, in her direct, emphatic, and focusing way, will immediately want to know about the exceptions. 'Under what special circumstances should we think of doing these things that are usually unthinkable for us?' And that, of course, is a question that we cannot answer and remain innocent. If philosophy makes me start thinking about the unthinkable in this sense, then philosophy quite literally 'robs me of my innocence'; very obviously, if the unthinkable is thought about, it is no longer unthinkable. (As Wittgenstein puts it in the Preface to the *Tractatus Logico-Philosophicus* (1921), 'In order to set a line as a limit to thought, it would be necessary to think both sides of that line.')

A lot of contemporary moral philosophy messes with our tacit knowledge, and that means it messes with our innocence. It messes with our tacit knowledge by pushing us into making explicit aspects of our moral sensibility that we had, until then, left unexplored – and (Williams and I would say) did better not to explore. If you are standing on a railway bridge next to a rather portly gentleman, and a railway disaster is unfolding on the lines below that seems to make it necessary to block one of them, will it even occur to you to push the fat man off the bridge to create this blockage? If you are normal, almost certainly not. But if you have read enough recent moral philosophy, almost certainly yes. Once the boundary between our explicit and our tacit knowledge is subjected to this sort of observation and interference, it is at least relocated, and perhaps destroyed altogether.

This too, then, is a process of observer interference, though of a very different kind from the describing-is-prescribing sort that I talked about in Chapter 3. At the limit of that process we could, in principle, lose our tacit knowledge altogether: we might come to live in a moral universe where nothing is literally unthinkable. Some moral philosophers – and above all, some utilitarians – apparently think that it might be a good thing to reach the limit of this process. Against them, I am contending that it would be a very bad thing indeed. And one way of saying what would be so bad about it, is to say that the further we go in that direction, the more we lose our innocence.

So good philosophy about friendship needs to recognise the importance of innocence. But here too, as before, the point is not that innocence is something we can't talk or think about. After all, I've just been talking about it. Nor is it that recognising innocence means becoming unable to do the philosophy of friendship altogether. Rather, the point is just that there are some trains of thought that friends will characteristically never even enter – will leave in what Williams, above, calls *deliberative silence*. Correspondingly, there are some lines of argument that the philosophy of friendship might do better not even to start on – it will leave them in what we might call *reflective silence*.

15 Moralism

We have seen that it is characteristic of a certain very popular style of contemporary moral philosophy to hold that there are no questions at all that philosophy should not ask. Those who take this line tend to see their stance as one of heroically bold and open-minded free thought. They apparently regard the contrary idea, which I have been defending by describing the virtue of innocence, as timid, no-debate obscurantism.

There is some irony in the fact that philosophers of this type tend to justify their ask-anything approach by appealing to science, given that the whole methodology of science rests on pursuing the right questions *and not the wrong ones*. But there is, anyway, more than one way for a question to be the wrong question to ask. We can pursue questions that fill our minds with horrible, grotesque imaginings that would never occur to us outside the philosophy seminar – and thereby lose our innocence. We can also pursue questions that presuppose the attitude, very common among philosophers, that I want to call *moralism*.

In its simplest form, moralism is simply another aspect of the kind of high-minded po-facedness that I was criticising at the start of Chapter 2: it is just being obsessed with the moral aspect of every issue. It means thinking that *everything is about morality* – about duties and prerogatives, about ought and may, about right and good. So, if we are going to talk philosophically about friendship, that must mean, first and foremost, thinking about the *duties* involved in friendship ('What ought a friend to do?') and the *rights* of a friend ('What is a friend allowed to do to/with me that no one else is?') and the *good* involved in friendship ('What is the value/benefit/point of friendship?').

It is not that these aren't good questions about friendship. I have already said that they are excellent questions; I have already spent a lot of time addressing them myself in this book. It is just that they are not the only questions about friendship, nor even, necessarily, the best questions to ask. If friendship is, as I have argued, an unemphatic good, then it is not likely that real-world friends will normally spend much time brow-clutching in a Wittgenstein-like way about their duties to each other, or take it to be central to their friendships that they have *rights* against their friends. Not at least in a healthy and flourishing friendship. For in truth, the moment you have to insist on your rights from a friend, the friendship itself is already in a crisis of some sort – its very continuance may be imperilled.

By and large, as I said above, the most characteristic thing for friends to be doing is not brow-clutching about anything, but 'messing about in boats' and other such forms of cheerful, unemphatic, and uncomplicated relaxation. Yet, as I've also noted, contemporary moral theory, when it turns to friendship, characteristically ignores all this. It focuses almost exclusively on heavily moralised questions about rights, duties, and the realisation of value, to the almost complete exclusion of any other questions about friendship.

So Kantian theorists tend to think that real friendship with anyone must be understood as friendship with Pure Reason Incarnate in that person. But this is an approach that risks losing sight of the unique particularity of any individual friend.

And as we saw in Chapter 2, utilitarian theorists tend to see friendships (and 'partiality' more generally) as suspect deviations from the direct maximisation of utility, deviations which are justifiable at all only because (and to the extent that), despite their indirectness, they indirectly bring about greater utility than more head-on approaches. But this is an approach that *holds friendship hostage*. Friendship – and partiality in general – is conceived as something *for which we need to have permission* from the 'janitors of the overall utility system' (as Williams (1973) acidly calls them), that is whoever it is that oversees the overall project of maximising the good. On this approach, getting leave to have friends is like getting a sick-note for school that lets you off Physical Education (PE), but only so you can recuperate for *future* PE lessons. You only get leave for the specific exemptions from maximising the good that your friendships involve, because *in the long run* granting you these exemptions will lead to greater utility.

In both these ways, moral theory in general – and not just its specific forms, such as utilitarianism and Kantianism – shows how strongly it is in the grip of moralism. The classic counter-attack on this sort of moralistic distortion of the nature of friendship is credited to Michael Stocker, whose justly famous article 'On the Schizophrenia of Modern Ethical Theories' points out how absurd it would be if we let such thoughts directly into our deliberations about what to do:

> Suppose you are in a hospital, recovering from a long illness. You are very bored and restless and at loose ends when Smith comes in ... You are ... convinced ... that he is a fine fellow and a real friend – taking so much time to cheer you up, travelling all the way across town, and so on. You are so effusive with your praise and thanks that he protests that he always tries to do what he thinks is his duty, what he thinks will be best. You at first think he is engaging in a polite form of self-deprecation, relieving the moral burden. But the more you two speak, the more clear it becomes that he was telling the literal truth: that it is not essentially because of you that he came to see you, not because you are friends, but because he thought it his duty, perhaps as a fellow Christian or Communist or whatever, or simply because he knows of no one more in need of cheering up and no one easier to cheer up. Surely there is something lacking here – and lacking in moral merit or value. (1976, 462)

Of course, we might possibly find another theoretical level to house such thoughts on. So the standard response in the literature to the absurdity that Stocker so vividly depicts is to withdraw the moralism from the level of deliberation to the level of justification. Sure, people say, it would be absurd for Smith to *deliberate* by way of thoughts about his duty, rather than by way of the friendly thoughts that it is (really) his duty to have. But when we come to *justify* how Smith deliberates, or should deliberate, then at this justificatory or reflective level we do need to invoke Kantian thoughts about respect for persons just as such, or utilitarian thoughts about what actions will maximise overall utility, or virtue-ethicist thoughts about which actions 'The Virtuous Person' would do – or whatever kind of justification is mandated by our preferred moral theory.

The trouble with this sort of move is, as Stocker already points out by way of his title, that it is hard to see how to mirror this theoretical division in any very convincing or attractive picture of our own psychology. The move induces a kind of schizophrenia, a kind of split vision, a kind of alienation from our own agency. On the one hand, we have all the *apparent* reasons why we do things, at the level of ordinary-life deliberations (to see my friends, to have fun together, to mess about on the river . . .). On the other hand, we have the *real* reasons why we do things, at the level of philosophical theory's justifications (to maximise utility, to respond to Practical Reason incarnate in others . . .). This split undermines the validity of our ordinary moral thinking. It says that ordinary moral thinking is *systematically mistaken*: our real reasons for action are quite other than what we normally think they are. It turns out, in short, to be a *debunking* view of ordinary ethical thought and action. We might also call it a patronising or condescending view, for on this view, no one else, no ordinary person, really understands what they are actually doing except for the moral theorist. And how the moral theorist keeps the peace in her own head, between thinking like an ordinary person and thinking like a moral theorist, is really rather hard to understand.

Much philosophical energy has been devoted to trying to repair this breakdown between moral theory and ethical practice. To my mind, the most successful attempts have focused on the clearly correct point that there has to be *some* room in our reflective thinking for a kind of distancing of ourselves from our own particular viewpoints. That is certainly true, but it need not imply what stronger versions of the 'two-level' view seem bound to imply – that ordinary moral thought, just as it stands, is systematically and fundamentally a web of illusions; that our *real* reasons for doing the right thing are never, or almost never, what they seem to be. In this kind of way, systematising moral theory can make us aliens to ourselves; this is one of the main reasons why I myself am an opponent of systematising moral theory. And the whole movement of thought away from our natural and intuitive patterns of deliberation and reflection does seem to be prompted, at least in part, by the basic mistake that I currently have in my sights: the mistake of moralism.

16 Roles and Spontaneity

In general, then, moralism in ethical philosophy means obsessively reducing everything we care about to ought and duty, right and wrong, permission and obligation. So moralism about friendship means doing this obsessive reduction in the specific case of friendship.

We have already listed some of the practical costs of moralism. One is the way it alienates us from our own lives and values – makes us stand outside who are and what we care about, to judge it from some distant standpoint. (A standpoint standing *where*, though? And with what authority? How could the view from anywhere else ever have ultimate deliberative or reflective priority, for me, over the view from where I am?) Another is the way it introduces anxiety and self-consciousness and emotional overload into what is naturally relaxed and unemphatic.

A third cost is the way moralism constantly refers us back to *what we ought to be doing*, making it seem that all our friendships are perpetually vulnerable to a kind of moral blackmail deriving from the constant possibility of overriding moral demands that wipe them out: 'How can I spend time hanging out with you when there is famine in Africa?' By filling our minds with such questions moralism uproots us from the innocent and natural spontaneity of the ordinary everyday good activities of our lives, including friendship, to a guilt-ridden focusing on things far away that we can't do very much about. I *don't* mean that we shouldn't try; I am *not* saying, 'Don't worry about those things' or 'Never mind about famine'. My point is that moralism uproots us, and that once we have been uprooted like this, it is very difficult to get back to where we were before. Re-engaging with ordinary goods like friendship under the aegis of the moral theorist's thought that there is (thank goodness!) a philosophical justification for those engagements is quite different from simply *engaging* with them. And arguably, less good.

In connection with this third threat, Bernard Williams sometimes writes of what he calls the 'obligation in, obligation out' principle: the idea that any moral obligation can be trumped or overridden by nothing but another, stronger obligation – so that if at any time we believe we have more reason to hang out with our friends than to rush off to join some famine-relief project, we can't be right in this belief unless we have a stronger obligation to hang out with our friends. (As Williams also puts it, 'the morality system . . . allows no emigration' (1985, 197).) This exchange of every kind of thought and reaction we have about value into the single currency of obligation is a classic move of moralism. It is a serious impoverishment of our ethical sensibility, and we should resist it.

Another connected way in which we are cheated and impoverished by moralism about friendship has to do, once more, with roles. It shouldn't be hard to see why moralistic thinking about roles creates problems for friendship. Of course we sometimes want to say, like Donkey in *Shrek*, that 'that's what friends do'. Sometimes there are things that we owe to each other just because we are friends: friendships *do* involve obligations, and Donkey's own example – forgiving our friends, sticking with them – is certainly one of the obligations that a friendship can involve. But suppose we were so caught up in moralistic thinking that we thought that friendship was a role that involved *nothing but* obligations. Or suppose we tried to list all and only the obligations involved in the role of friendship. It should be pretty obvious that this would not be a terribly fruitful line of inquiry, and would be unlikely to produce any very clear or convincing list of those obligations.

In any case, what could we do with such a list? We might use our list of the obligations of the role of friendship to berate ourselves. I might say, 'I claim to be John's friend, but being a friend means listening properly, and last night when he wanted to talk to me I didn't listen at all – my bad.' But now switch this round, and suppose John tries to use the same kind of appeal to berate *me*: 'You claim to be my friend, but I need someone to talk to, and you're the only one around, and you won't listen.' Sometimes an appeal like this will work, but in general such appeals are very easy to shrug off. One simple and popular way to get rid of them is just to reject the idea that we have this obligation in the first place. (As Russell must sometimes have been tempted to say to Wittgenstein: 'Well, if being your friend means having to listen to the nonsense you're talking tonight, then I suppose I'm not your friend after all.')

In general, attempts like this to commandeer some-one's friendship, or to frog-march or arm-lock them into particular kinds of action or response 'because you are my friend', is going to come across as a highly objectionable kind of moral blackmail. What friends give each other in their friendship, they are supposed to give *for free*, cheerfully, and without any need for psychological strong-arm tactics or making a martyred fuss about it. To make the demand that someone should do something because they are my friend, and because doing it is part of the role of friendship – this is like carpeting your boyfriend on the morning of Valentine's Day and demanding to see his card for you. Such moralistic appeals to clearly defined roles fail to respect the freely-givenness of friendship. If you make just one such appeal, it will almost certainly have a bad effect on your friendship. If you do it repeatedly, the friendship is very likely not to survive at all. It's not that friendship *isn't* a role; it's not that the role of friendship brings no duties with it. It's just that there is something peculiarly self-defeating about insisting upon the performance of these duties. For they were supposed to happen – that word again – *spontaneously*. And where there is this kind of insistence, there can be no spontaneity.

Friendship is certainly a role. But friendship *as such* is quite a vague and amorphous role, and a lot of the slack involved in the role of friend is taken up by other roles that we occupy. So equally certainly, compared with the more demanding and precise notions of friendship that other societies have sometimes had, friendship as such is not a well-defined role *in our society*. We certainly recognise that *particular* friendships can be roles, with particular obligations and duties understood to be part of them (but only part – against the moralist, I want to keep on insisting that there is always more to any friendship than the obligations it involves).

We also recognise that there are kinds of standing that overlap with being a friend that are also roles, and that often a lot of the duties involved in these friendships come from those other roles. For example, sisters can be friends, as Lizzy and Jane Bennet are, and being a sister is certainly a role in a fairly tight sense. Or again, colleagues can be friends, as Lightwood and Wrayburn are (Dickens 1865); professional colleague is another role. There is a vague general role of friendship, and some vague general list of concomitant duties. But in truth many of the duties that are supposedly part of the role of friendship are either duties that come from being a sister, or a colleague, or a neighbour, or a fellow member of the congregation, and so forth. Or they are really duties that we owe to anyone, not because they are our friends, but simply because they are other human beings. (As John Skorupksi has pointed out to me: when people say, as they often do, 'We shouldn't betray our friends', it seems a perfectly fair retort to reply, 'Well, no. But then, you shouldn't betray *anybody*.')

The most basic reason why friendship *as such* is a pretty vague role – as opposed to particular types of friendship, or particular individual friendships – is very simply because friendship as such is a pretty vague thing. There hardly *is* any such thing as 'friendship as such': there are just particular friendships, particular kinds of affectionate attachment between individuals. And those particularities vary *enormously*. Being a friend can involve deathbed scenes, as it does for Lightwood and Wrayburn in *Our Mutual*

Friend (Dickens 1865); it can involve restraining and temporarily imprisoning your friend till he finds his right mind, as Ratty, Mole, and Badger do to Toad in *The Wind in the Willows* (Grahame 1908); it can even involve shooting him, as happens in Steinbeck's *Of Mice and Men* (1937). Friendships can be between sisters and brothers, young and old, grandparents and grandchildren (my own grandfather was one of my first best friends), different races and castes and classes and religions (think of Maan Kapoor and Firoz Khan in *A Suitable Boy* (Seth 1993)), between clever people and people who aren't clever at all (Lenny and George in *Of Mice and Men* again). Friends can be temporary or permanent, face to face or epistolary (like Cicero and Atticus), present or distant, people you see in just one context or people with whom you share your whole life; friends can also be members of other species, like Rai Gaita's dog (2003), or Mark Rowlands' wolf (2008), or Gavin Maxwell's otters (1960).

I could list plenty of further variations in what friendships can be, but this is enough examples to make the simple point. Beyond the basic commonality of affectionate attachment between individuals over time, there need be next to nothing else that all friendships have in common. And so, there is next to nothing else that they all have in common, in the way of obligations and duties deriving from the role of the friend. Moreover, it could be constraining and constricting to insist that they must have more than this in common; it might actually be more fruitful to *allow* all this present diversity – and leave the door open too to even more possible diversity in the future. It is an important part of the spontaneity of friendship – and of love in general – that we accept the givenness of the other, that we allow our friend to be different from anything we might have prescribed or predicted. It is an equally important part of the spontaneity of friendship that we allow the relationship itself to be given in this way: to develop in directions that we never laid down, and could not have dreamed of in advance. As I pointed out in Chapter 10, friendship involves vulnerability and risk, of kinds that we can never experience with a bot-friend or a robot lover. And that, after all, is kind of the point of friendship. Because it involves a real other person, friendship is not just in our heads. And the most real and valuable friendships are never entirely within our control.

We've seen how moralism can weaponise the idea of friendship as a role in order to subvert our friendships, and with them our innocence, our spontaneity, and the legitimate role of tacit knowledge in our moral awareness and reflection. That is one good reason why we should be wary of treating friendship as a single general role of any very clear and specific shape. To do so risks being unduly confining and restricting. We should keep our minds open to *new* possibilities about what any particular friendship might involve. Because one of the most notable and attractive things of all about friendship is this: that it is always open to the future.

17   The Benefits of Friendship

So far in this book I have raised lots of questions about friendship. I have said something about the nature of friendship. I have considered some of the most famous philosophical theorists of friendship, and looked at just a few of the many works of philosophy, art, and literature where friendships are important or central. I have said something about the way in which a key part of the delight of friendship, much of the time, is how unemphatic, unselfconscious, tacit, innocent, spontaneous, and unmoralistic it is.

So – if we can ask the question without getting too emphatic and self-conscious, and also without getting too instrumental – what are the benefits of friendship? What good does it do us to have friends?

That is the question I shall ask in this penultimate chapter. In the very last chapter, as promised earlier, I shall provide a very quick Q&A on a list of eighteen questions about friendship, just to give a kind of rapid summary of where (if anywhere) the argument of this book has got us to, and just to appease those who like their philosophy neat rather than untidy. Whether such neatness is ever really as conclusive as it may look, or really just rooted in an arbitrariness that untidiness does not share when untidiness is untidy *in response to the evidence* ... that question is, of course, entirely another matter.

(This book's structure gives a certain prominence to the number 18. Do I have some deep cabbalistic, mystical justification for this use of 18? I do not. If I am making any point by doing a number of things in eighteens, it is more likely that I am mocking the pretensions of over-tidy philosophy.)

How then does friendship benefit us? The short answer is that the benefits of friendship go all the way 'up the scale' of what it is to be human, from what is most animal and zoological in us, to what is most rational and spiritual: all the way from the ape to the angel. (So if Aristotle's point was that human motivations go from the lowest kind, 'pleasure and money', via 'honour', up to the highest kind, towards 'virtue and the good', then at least I agree with him that friendship has something to offer us at all these levels – even if I don't agree with his way of dividing up the levels.)

In this chapter I am going to list seven benefits of friendship in particular. (My apologies that I couldn't think of another eleven to get us up to eighteen. Seven is a rather mystical number too, of course.)

At the lowest level of our natures and of friendship, there is the very basic phenomenon, first mentioned in Chapter 6, of *animal compresence*, of simply being the kind of creature that enjoys having other animals around. Think of Simon and Garfunkel's 'old friends, sharing a park bench like book ends'. (What a pity that Simon and Garfunkel did not manage to stay friends themselves.) Or think of a dog and his human, curled up together in front of a blazing fire. Or of twin babies who fall asleep together, with no idea why they like each other's company, but a very clear sense that they do. Or of long-married couples who can and do spend an evening very contentedly reading different books. They don't ever feel the least need to entertain each other or to dazzle in conversation, and on the face of it they might almost seem, to an unreflective observer or to someone who has imbibed too many popular images of 'romance', to be ignoring each other. Yet they are deeply together, and each would miss the other enormously if they were not there. (Unemphaticness again; see Chapter 5.)

If friendship with God is possible, then maybe even that most hard-to-imagine kind of friendship can, paradoxically enough, include something like animal compresence. There is the familiar anecdote of the old peasant who spends hours in front of the altar; his priest asks him what words he is praying while he sits there, and the old man replies 'Words? No.' 'What then?' says the priest. 'I sits and looks at Him,' answers the old man, 'and He looks back at me.'

Of course, part of the pleasure of animal compresence is the thought – which we may or may not ever get round to making explicit – that someone else enjoys my company enough to want to share it (even if all we are doing to share each other's company is sleeping in the same bed, or dozing in front of the same fire). Along with the compresence of other humans there comes – usually – some affirming reassurance that *somebody likes me*, that I am not an entirely horrible or boring or worthless person to spend time with. (And not just humans: if someone wanted to design an animal specifically to make us feel loved, they would probably design something pretty much like a dog.)

This reassurance that somebody likes me is the second benefit of friendship that I'll list here: the sense of *affirmation* that friendship can give us. This second benefit itself subdivides: it comes in a variety of forms. Three prominent forms are affirmation as *liking*, affirmation as *respect*, and affirmation as *admiration*. To be liked by others is to have some reason to think that I *can* attract affection (because apparently I do). To be respected is to be confirmed in the view that my interests and my rights deserve protection and enforcement (because apparently others are protecting and enforcing my interests and my rights). And for me to be admired is for me to be seen as deserving of honour for my abilities or achievements (because if I am admired, then apparently others do see me as deserving of honour). Affirmation is a very various thing, and it too has levels and forms that go much of the way 'up the scale' of what it is to be human; these are just three of them. Friendship in its various forms helps to provide us with all of these forms of affirmation, and others.

So at the level of affection, it is a matter of obvious fact, and of psychiatric fact too, that there are few things more healing for any damaged psyche than simply knowing that one is loved. And at the level of respect, it is equally important to know that someone thinks my interests and rights are worth defending. All members of oppressed minorities know how hard it is to go on believing in yourself, and in your own right to exist, in a society that seems intent on mocking and belittling you, and on denying that right. It is not, if you are in that minority, that you don't believe in yourself and your rights; it is just that it is so much easier to believe when you aren't surrounded by haters shouting in your face, but by allies – or even friends.

At the level of respect, what friendship gives us – though certainly, it needs to be the friendship of good people! – is in a way the opposite of what is called 'gaslighting'. It is a mark of bad people that they skew others' moral perceptions: they make me see myself in a falsely bad light, and them in a falsely good one. The gaslighting of bad people is cancelled out by the affirming respect of good people. They tell me that, in fact, despite all the jeering trolls who have been in my face so long, I am *not* a disgusting monster, or a bizarre freak, or a pointlessly tedious insect. And it does me a huge amount of good to hear them saying so, and to believe them when they say it.

Provided they're right, of course. Friends do have the role of helping us calibrate our moral compasses, and that includes telling us when we've got it right. At the same time and by the same token, it also includes telling us when we've got it wrong. As Sir Francis Bacon notes in his essay 'Of Friendship':

> ... there is no such flatterer as is a man's self; and there is
> no such remedy against flattery of a man's self, as the
> liberty of a friend. Counsel is of two sorts: the one
> concerning manners, the other concerning business. For
> the first, the best preservative to keep the mind in health,
> is the faithful admonition of a friend. The calling of a
> man's self to a strict account, is a medicine, sometime too
> piercing and corrosive. Reading good books of morality,
> is a little flat and dead. Observing our faults in others, is
> sometimes improper for our case. But the best receipt

(best, I say, to work, and best to take) is the admonition
of a friend. It is a strange thing to behold, what gross
errors and extreme absurdities many (especially of the
greater sort) do commit, for want of a friend to tell
them ... (before 1626, n. p.)

At the level of honour, we move on to a third benefit
of friendship. Whatever else we might disagree with in *The
Four Loves*, C. S. Lewis (1960) was on to something when he
said that it is emblematic of lovers to face each other, but of
friends to face a third thing together. The third benefit that
friendship offers is *partnership*, meaning that it is characteristic of at least some friends to engage in projects together,
skilled activities of various kinds, many of them being projects where a partner is not just helpful but essential
(climbing with a rope, for instance).

A good partnership is characterised by mutual
admiration, but in a good way: in a good sense of that
usually pejorative phrase, which brings us back to the notion
of second-personality that I talked about in Chapter 10.
Partners teach each other how to do what they do together,
whether that is skiing or acting or music-making or philosophy or running a business. They learn from each other and
compete with each other (though not too fiercely, unless
their partnership is going a bit sour). They challenge and
push each other to do better. The craft is everything, and
they are co-labourers in it. And when things go well, then, as
I say, they admire each other, and with good reason. 'We
couldn't get up this without Skip's sailing skills, without
Crag's determination and zest and make-do-and-mend
ingenuity, without Stephen's ability to dig in and survive in

an Antarctic storm, or without Simon's unmatched ability to lead steep, precarious, and poorly protected mixed climbing ... we have *all* brought something to the table': this is the kind of mutual honouring characteristic of partners in a shared endeavour. (I am thinking of a particular mountaineering partnership, the first ascent of Starbuck Peak in South Georgia in 2016, which involved two personal friends of whom I am unendingly envious (and admiring), Simon Richardson and Stephen Venables; see the interview with them on www.ukclimbing.com, titled 'Venables and Richardson on South Georgia'.)

The sheer variety of the benefits that friendship can bring us should be obvious here too, given the sheer variety of possible partnerships. We climb mountains together, or we do yoga together, or we form knitting circles together, or we put clothes together to sell together, or we plot the downfall of the oppressor together, or (like Russell and Ogden in Chapter 12) we think about mathematical logic together. There can be partnerships in things that go all the way 'up the scale' of what it is to be human, from what is most zoological in us, to what is most rational. (Or, for that matter, all the way down the scale.)

Such participation in joint enterprises has a feature that is not unique to those friendships that involve partnership, but which it does bring out particularly clearly. This is a fourth benefit of pretty well any friendship, which is found in friendship's close relationship with our experience of time. In a longstanding friendship we share a present, on the basis of a shared past, and with a shared but open future to come. Present future, past memory, and anticipation and excitement about the future are all part of it: friendships are, as we might say, dynamic through *shared time*.

The same variety is obvious when we turn to a fifth benefit of friendship, namely that it gives us someone to *share experiences with*. The variety here is the variety of possible experiences; under this heading of 'experience' we might find the sharing of a prison sentence or a war, but also the sharing of a mountaineering expedition, or child-raising, or a mathematical discovery – or of what, in previous work, I have called an *epiphany*. This last possibility, of sharing an epiphany, seems to be what Archytas of Tarentum is talking about in the Prelude's very first aphorism.

Saying that we *share* such experiences involves variety too: we share an experience in one sense if we go through it together, but we share it in another if you go through it and then tell me about it (or vice versa). There is also, as Sir Francis Bacon points out, the service that friends provide for us when they listen to our troubles:

> A principal fruit of friendship, is the ease and discharge of the fullness and swellings of the heart, which passions of all kinds do cause and induce. We know diseases of stoppings, and suffocations, are the most dangerous in the body; and it is not much otherwise in the mind; you may take sarza to open the liver, steel to open the spleen, flowers of sulphur for the lungs, castoreum for the brain; but no receipt openeth the heart, but a true friend; to whom you may impart griefs, joys, fears, hopes, suspicions, counsels, and whatsoever lieth upon the heart to oppress it, in a kind of civil shrift or confession. (before 1626, n. p.)

Alongside all these benefits that we can receive from our friends there is a further and subtler benefit: as well as them benefiting us, we benefit *them* – and it is a benefit to us to benefit them. It is good to have a good listener to talk to. But it is also good to be *trusted* to be a good listener. It is good to care for others, but it is good, too, to have others to care for. It is good to have others' encouragement and support, but it is also a benefit to me to be someone on whom others rely for encouragement and support. It is not only, in the words of the old jazz song, to have 'someone to watch over me'; it is also to have someone whom I can watch over. In all these ways we are benefited by our friends, simply inasmuch as we find we are able to benefit them.

A cynic might describe this sort of phenomenon in egotistical terms, as 'feeding our sense of importance', and there is certainly a danger to beware of there. But we might, less cynically, and more accurately, speak of it as feeding our sense of significance. *Being needed by others* can of course become pathological and/or egotistical. But when it doesn't, it is a natural and deep kind of benefit not only to the needy one, but also to the one who is needed.

This kind of *mutuality* is a sixth benefit of friendship that we all hope for, and value greatly when it comes our way. One lesson that mutuality has to teach us is that it is not as easy as we might think, if we are readers of Nygren, to tell need-love from gift-love. For one of the deepest gifts that we can give to others is to entrust them with our own needs, and one of our deepest needs is to be, ourselves, needed.

So mutuality brings us to the seventh and last benefit of friendship that anyone might hope to attain from engaging in it. This benefit is *the remaking of our notion of benefit*. What friendship can teach me to do is to stop thinking of *my* benefit at all, and learn to think instead of *our* benefit. My good turns into *our* good; my reasons for acting become *our* reasons for acting; each *I* becomes a part of a larger *we*. Any individual has the best of individual reasons to become part of a fellowship of friends in this way, but to do so is to move beyond the very idea of individual reasons, into the realm of shared reasons.

Such moves to the collective level, to the level at which our reasons become shared reasons, are never irreversible or all-pervasive. And as is no doubt obvious, they are always profoundly risky. But when things work out well with them, when a friendship truly becomes both a shared good and a shared pursuit of shared goods, then nothing in the world is more worthwhile.

18 Eighteen Quick Questions and Eighteen Quick Answers

1 What is the definition of friendship?

There isn't a logically watertight formal definition. And the fact that we can't formally define friendship teaches us some important lessons about the nature of philosophical inquiry – lessons that we have (or should have) been learning ever since Plato, and that Wittgenstein helps to remind us of. But loosely and roughly, and without any promise of counter-example-proofness: friendship is benevolent companionship over time. Here what I mean by 'companionship' involves *mutual second-personality*: it means that I see someone else as a person who sees me as a person.

2 Is friendship a role, and a thick ethical concept?

Friendship is a role, yes, in a general way. But the looseness of the definition of friendship, and the very wide range of different things that friendship can be (and in different times and places has been), transmits into a looseness in the definition of the role of friendship. This looseness is a good thing; it gives us room to be creative about what friendship is to be *for us, starting from here*.

And yes, friendship is a thick ethical concept too. Thick ethical concepts are *bridging* concepts, concepts that link possible courses of action in the world, via particular institutions or traditions or practices or dispositions in the world, to moral verdicts. And friendship is certainly a concept like that – though again, exactly how it does this bridging is a constitutively vague matter, because friendship is a constitutively vague concept and role, which (see next question) generates correspondingly vague duties.

3 What are the duties of friendship?

The looseness in the definition of the role of friendship means that the duties of friendship are not at all clearly defined. Some of them are not really duties to *friends* at all, but simply to fellow human beings (or just fellow beings). Others are duties that arise within a *particular* friendship, but because of its particular nature, not because of the nature of friendship *in general*. The duties of friendship as such are things like loyalty and particular attention. But how demanding these duties are is not something that can be defined in general: I don't owe the same loyalty and particular attention to a casual work acquaintance and to my spouse.

4 How do examples of friendship help?

By feeding our imaginations with particular, detailed, and credible stories about what friendship actually involves (either in fiction or in the real world). In that sense a list of examples, like mine, or the OED's, or Plato's characters Meno's and Theaetetus', is not a distraction from getting clear about the concept of friendship, but a key part of getting clear.

5 How does a natural history of friendship help?

By reminding us that friendship, if it is anything at all, is a part of the natural life of our biological species (and other species too).

6 Is friendship a type of love?

Certainly – though there isn't just one way of counting the types of love.

7 Can lovers/spouses be friends?

Yes, of course. Friendship is benevolent companionship over time, so if marriage or lifelong partnership is anything good at all, then one good thing that it will certainly be is a kind of friendship.

8 Can parents and children be friends? Can animals? Can God?

Yes, for very similar reasons to (7).

9 Can we be friends with the inanimate world?

Not literally, perhaps. Friendship is benevolent companionship over time, and companionship involves *mutual second-personality*: that is, it means that I see someone else as a person who sees me as a person. The inanimate world doesn't do this, not literally, except on pantheistic views of the world that the present writer, at any rate, doesn't share: when I look at the woods and the fields, the woods and the fields do not literally *look back at me*. However, it is certainly possible for me to have a particular long-term affection for, say, a particular wood or river or mountain or landscape, and to feel that I get far more good from it than I am ever capable of repaying, and to feel even that I am, in some sense, *held to account* by that landscape: it waits for me; it makes demands of me; it asks me questions; it is (like Galadriel's mirror) a stillness into which I may look, and see some peace come to the turmoil of my own mind. This is something that many of us experience with the inanimate natural world. (It is closely connected with what I have to say in *Epiphanies* 4.4 (Chappell 2022b) about our sense of place.)

10 Can we be friends with ourselves?

Yes and no. The requirements for mutual second-personality are almost, but not quite, fulfilled by the reflexive case. I can certainly see myself as 'a person who sees me as a person'. But this is, *ex hypothesi*, not seeing someone *else* this way.

But perhaps people don't mean quite that anyway, when they say that it is a good thing to be friends with yourself. What they mean is that you should be forgiving and tolerant and accepting and encouraging of and gentle with yourself. Which you should, of course.

11 Do friendships have to be with equals, or with similars?

No, definitely not. All children (who are not orphans or otherwise deprived) have vital relationships with their parents that are certainly friendship in my sense of 'benevolent companionship over time', and without which they could not learn how to live with other human beings at all. If equality or similarity was a prerequisite for friendship, perhaps we could never get started on learning that: there would be no way into the circle. And certainly our world and our lives would be hugely impoverished; there is so much to learn from those who are *not at all* like us.

What tends to push people – especially high-achieving men like C. S. Lewis and Aristotle – into requiring equality for friendship is first their close involvement with other high-achieving men like themselves, and secondly their regrettable tendency to be forgetful of the circumstances in which we all begin as, in Alasdair MacIntyre's (1999) fine words, 'dependent rational animals'. Perhaps it is easier for a woman to avoid this kind of forgetfulness of our own dependency than for a man.

12 Is friendship unfair?

Some philosophers think so; they think that friendship involves unjust impartiality towards some at the expense of others. This is a misunderstanding of friendship, and indeed of impartiality. Not everything is subject to the impartialist demand of equal treatment, and it is not the nature of life for us to be even-handed distributors of well-being to everyone around us. It is a deep mistake of utilitarianism, at least in its more direct forms, to think so.

The worst of this utilitarian mistake is that it tends to deprive us of the benefits of friendship, especially those that depend on second-personality and the remaking of our notion of benefit: see Chapter 17.

13 Can a bad person be a good friend?

It rather depends. For a start, it depends on whether we are asking whether they can be good friends *with a good person*, or good friends *with another bad person*. Friendship involves kindness, generosity, trust, honesty, and the like; these are virtues (characteristics of good people), not vices (characteristics of bad people). But up to a point, even bad people can display these virtues to each other. So yes, up to a point they can.

14 Can a good person be a bad friend?

This is easier. The answer is clearly Yes. To a bad person, a good person *should* be 'a bad friend', if that means not going along with or endorsing or facilitating their badness. We are too easily drawn by our desire to be liked by others into not challenging their bad behaviour. Of course a good person (as such) will not be unkind or mean or treacherous or dishonest, nor overly moralistic or judgemental. But sometimes it is right to drop a friendship because keeping it up would mean becoming (or becoming an accomplice to) a racist, or a thief, or a bully, or whatever else.

15 When is it right to start a friendship?

Whenever you like, and ideally before you have formulated this question. Friendship is an unemphatic good, and that is particularly true of its beginnings. Much better if they are spontaneous rather than contrived, unemphatic rather than laboured, tacit rather than self-conscious.

16 When is it right to end a friendship?

Besides what I say above under (14), there are the claims of loyalty to consider. As Donkey points out to Shrek, the whole point of having a friendship is that it means that there is someone whom I can rely on to stick by me *even if I am not currently great company.* How far are we obliged to take this 'sticking with' others? Quite a long way, but not an infinite distance. People can, alas, become impossibly objectionable: Shrek always was like that before the film started, and gets perilously close to being like that in it, too.

Again, people can become *bad* people when they weren't before. Somewhere down such lines of development, it becomes reasonable – and sometimes imperative – to break off a friendship. Exactly where is not something about which we can make a general statement. It depends on the details of the case – on whether, in the spirit of Aristotle's doctrine of the mean, we need to keep more of an eye on ourselves for moroseness than for easy-going over-familiarity, or vice versa, and on *phronesis*, good ethical judgement.

17 Can we be happy without friends?

Probably. All sorts of things are *possible*, in one sense or another of that protean word. But most of us won't be. The benefits of friendship are too considerable, and too central to what it is to be human, for that to be at all likely: see (18).

18 What are the benefits of friendship?

See Chapter 17. The benefits of friendship are pretty well everything.

REFERENCES

Note: Quotes from works by Aristotle, Dante Alighieri, Plato, Homer, and William Shakespeare have been drawn from various online sources, of which many are easily accessible.

Abramson Kate, and Adam Leite, 2011. 'Love as a Reactive Emotion.' *The Philosophical Quarterly* 61 (245): 673–699.

The Advent Project. n.d. 'Gregory of Nazianzus: Why It Matters That God Become Human.' Available at https://theadventusproject .wordpress.com/resources/sermons-and-devotions/why-it-matters-that-god-become-human-gregory-of-nazianzus/.

Appiah, Kwame Anthony. 1994. 'Identity, Authenticity, Survival.' *Multiculturalism*, edited by A. Gutmann, 149–164. Princeton: Princeton University Press.

Augustine. (413 AD) 1912. *Confessions*. Loeb parallel text, tr. William Watts. Cambridge, MA: Harvard University Press.

Austen, Jane. 1813. *Pride and Prejudice*. London: T. Egerton.

Bacon, Sir Francis. Before 1626. 'Of Friendship.' Available at www.authorama.com/essays-of-francis-bacon-27.html.

Beauvoir, Simone de. (1949) 1972. *The Second Sex*. Tr. H. M. Parshley, London: Penguin.

Blake, William. 1804. *Jerusalem*. Available at https://en.wikisource .org/wiki/Jerusalem._The_Emanation_of_the_Giant_Albion.

Chappell, Sophie Grace. 2021. *Songs For Winter Rain*. Durham: Ellipsis Imprints.

Chappell, Sophie Grace. 2022a. 'Anscombe's Three Theses.' *Handbook to the Philosophy of Elizabeth Anscombe*, edited by Roger Teichmann, 91–117. Oxford: Oxford University Press.

Chappell, Sophie Grace. 2022b. *Epiphanies*. Oxford: Oxford University Press.

Chappell, Sophie Grace. 2024. *Trans Figured: On Being a Transgender Person in a Cisgender World*. Cambridge: Polity.

Chappell, Timothy. 2001. 'Option Ranges.' *Journal of Applied Philosophy* 18 (2): 107–118.

Chappell, Timothy. 2003. *Reading Plato's Theaetetus*. Minneapolis: Hackett.

Chappell, Timothy, ed. 2009. *The Problem of Moral Demandingness: New Philosophical Essays*. London: Palgrave Macmillan.

Chappell, Timothy. 2013. 'There Are No Thin Concepts.' *Thick Concepts*, edited by Simon Kirchin, 182–196. Mind Association Occasional Series. Oxford: Oxford University Press.

Cicero. (50 BC) 1958. *de Amicitia*. Loeb parallel text, tr. W. Falconer. Cambridge, MA: Harvard University Press.

Confucius. (200 AD) 1958. *Analects*. Tr. D. C. Lau. London: Penguin Classics.

Davies, Robertson. 1981. *The Rebel Angels*. London: Macmillan.

Dickens, Charles. 1865. *Our Mutual Friend*. London: Chapman and Hall.

Douglas, Mary. 1966. *Purity and Danger*. London: Routledge.

Driver, Julia. 1989. 'The Virtues of Ignorance.' *The Journal of Philosophy* 86 (7): 373–384.

Emerson, Ralph Waldo. n.d. 'Friendship.' Available at www.literaturepage.com/read/emersonessays1-104.html; www.literaturepage.com/read/emersonessays1-108.html.

Fermor, Patrick Leigh. 1957. *A Time To Keep Silence*. London: Penguin.

Forster, E. M. 1939. 'What I Believe.' Available at forsem0001whabel.pdf.

Gaita, Rai. 2003. *The Philosopher's Dog*. London: Routledge.

Gartner, Corinne. 2022. 'Aristotle on the Nature and Value of Friendship.' *The Routledge Handbook of the Philosophy of Friendship*, edited by Diane Jeske, 35–46. London: Routledge.

Grahame, Kenneth. 1908. *The Wind in the Willows*. London: Methuen.

Grice, H. P. 1957. 'Meaning.' *The Philosophical Review* 66 (3): 377–388.

Herodotus, 430 BC. *The Histories*. Available at https://www.perseus.tufts.edu/hopper/text?doc=Perseus:text:1999.01.0126.

Hinds, Marcus. 2016. 'C. S. Lewis on Anders Nygren: "He Has Shaken Me Up Extremely" by Dr Jason Lepojärvi, St Benet's Hall, Oxford.' Cambridge Core, 6 July 2016. https://www.cambridge.org/core/blog/2016/07/06/c-s-lewis-on-anders-nygren-he-has-shaken-me-up-extremely-by-dr-jason-lepojarvi-st-benets-hall-oxford/.

Hornby, Nick. 1995. *High Fidelity*. London: Penguin.

Hughes, Thomas. 1857. *Tom Brown's Schooldays*. London: Macmillan.

John, Jeffrey. 2001. *The Meaning in the Miracles*. Norwich: Canterbury Press.

Johnson, Samuel. Johnson's Dictionary Online. Available at johnsonsdictionaryonline.com.

Jollimore, Troy. 2011. *Love's Vision*. Princeton: Princeton University Press.

Kant, Immanuel. (1797) 2017. *Groundwork for the Metaphysics of Morals*. Tr. Mary Gregor. Cambridge: Cambridge University Press.

Kaye, Kenneth. 1982. *The Mental and Social Life of Babies: How Parents Create Persons*. Chicago: University of Chicago Press.

Lewis, C. S. 1960. *The Four Loves*. London: Geoffrey Bles.

Lewis, C. S. 1961. *A Grief Observed*. London: Faber.

McGuinness, Brian. 1988. *Wittgenstein: A Life*. London: Duckworth.

185

MacIntyre, Alasdair. 1999. *Dependent Rational Animals: Why Human Beings Need the Virtues*. London: Duckworth.

Maxwell, Gavin. 1960. *Ring of Bright Water*. London: Penguin.

Mill, John Stuart. 1859. 'On Liberty.' Available at https://socialsciences.mcmaster.ca/econ/ugcm/3ll3/mill/liberty.pdf.

Monk, Ray. 1990. *Ludwig Wittgenstein: The Duty of Genius*. New York: Free Press.

Montaigne, Michel de. 1580. 'Of Friendship.' Available at https://www.gutenberg.org/files/3600/3600-h/3600-h.htm.

Murdoch, Iris. 1970. *The Sovereignty of Good*. London: Routledge.

Murdoch, Iris. 1999. *Existentialists & Mystics*. Collected essays, edited by Peter Conradi. London: Pengun.

Nehamas, Alexander. 2016. *On Friendship*. New York: Basic Books.

Nietzsche, Friedrich. 1883–1885. *Thus Spake Zarathustra*. Available at https://www.gutenberg.org/files/1998/1998-h/1998-h.htm.

Nietzsche, Friedrich. (1887) 2013. *On The Genealogy of Morals*. London: Penguin.

Nygren, Anders. 1930. *Agape och Eros*. English translation, *Agape and Eros*, in 1953. London: Chatto and Windus.

Parfit, Derek. 1984. *Reasons and Persons*. Oxford: Oxford University Press.

Polanyi, Michael. 1958. *Personal Knowledge: Towards a Post-Critical Philosophy*. London: Routledge and Kegan Paul.

Rawls, John. 1971. *A Theory of Justice*. New York: Oxford University Press.

Rawls, John. 1993. *Political Liberalism*. New York: Columbia University Press.

Rousseau, Jean-Jacques. (1762) 1913. *du Contrat Social (The Social Contract)*. Available at https://oll.libertyfund.org/title/cole-the-social-contract-and-discourses.

Rowlands, Mark. 2008. *The Philosopher and the Wolf*. London: Granta.

Russell, Bertrand. 1912. 'The Problems of Philosophy.' Available at
www.gutenberg.org/files/5827/5827-h/5827-h.htm.

Russell, Bertrand. 1959. *My Philosophical Development*. London:
George Allen & Unwin.

Russell, Bertrand. 1967. *Autobiography*. London: Routledge.

Sandel, Michael. 1994. 'Review of John Rawls, *Political Liberalism*.'
Harvard Law Review 107: 1765–1794.

Schliesser, Eric. 2023. 'Good Breeding, Population Ethics and All
That: On MacAskills's What We Owe the Future, Part 4.'
Crooked Timber, 13 January 2023. Available at https://
crookedtimber.org/2023/01/13/50828/.

Scott, Walter. 1805. 'The Lay of the Last Minstrel.' Available at e
www.theotherpages.org/poems/minstrel.html.

Seth, Vikram. 1993. *A Suitable Boy*. London: Weidenfeld &
Nicolson.

Shelton SJ, Charles. 1975. 'Friendship in the Jesuit Life.' *Studies in
the Spirituality of Jesuits* 27 (5).

Sparrow, John. 1981. *Grave Epigrams and Other Verses*. London:
Cygnet Press.

Steinbeck, John. 1937. *Of Mice and Men*. United States: Covici
Friede.

Stocker, Michael. 1976. 'On the Schizophrenia of Modern Ethical
Theories.' *Journal of Philosophy* 73 (14): 453–466.

Stohr, Karen. 2022. *Choosing Freedom*. New York: Oxford
University Press.

Strawson, Peter. 1962. 'Freedom and Resentment.' *Proceedings of
the British Academy* 48: 187–211.

Velleman, David. 1999. 'Love as a Moral Emotion.' *Ethics* 109 (2):
338–374.

Whillans, Geoffrey, and Ronald Searle. 1954. *How to Be Topp*.
London: Max Parrish.

White, T. H. 1958. *The Once and Future King*. London:
Collins.

Wilde, Oscar. 1894. 'A Few Maxims for the Instruction of the Over-Educated.' Available at https://www.themarginalian.org/2014/10/16/oscar-wilde-a-few-maxims-for-the-instruction-of-the-over-educated/.

Williams, Bernard. 1973. 'A Critique of Utilitarianism.' *Utilitarianism: For and Against*, edited by J. C. C. Smart and Bernard Williams, 68–128. Oxford: Blackwell.

Williams, Bernard. 1981. *Moral Luck*. Cambridge: Cambridge University Press.

Williams, Bernard. 1985. *Ethics and the Limits of Philosophy*. London: Penguin.

Williamson, Timothy. 2007. *The Philosophy of Philosophy*. Oxford: Blackwell.

Wittgenstein, Ludwig. 1921. *Tractatus Logico-Philosophicus*. London: Routledge.

Wittgenstein, Ludwig. 1951. *Philosophical Investigations*. Oxford: Blackwell.

Wittgenstein, Ludwig. 1958. *The Blue and Brown Books*. Oxford: Blackwell.

Wittgenstein, Ludwig. 1969. *On Certainty*. Oxford: Blackwell.

Wittgenstein, Ludwig. 1971. *Prototractatus*, edited by B. McGuinness et al. London: Routledge.

INDEX

189